VIETNAM
in Pictures

Stacy Taus-Bolstad

Lerner Publications Company

Contents

Website address: www.lernerbooks.com

Lerner Publications Company
A division of Lerner Publishing Group
241 First Avenue North
Minneapolis, MN 55401 U.S.A.

Library of Congress Cataloging-in-Publication Data

Taus-Bolstad, Stacy.
        Vietnam in pictures / by Stacy Taus-Bolstad.—Rev. & expanded.
        p.   cm. — (Visual geography series)
        Summary: Text and illustrations present detailed information on the geography, history and
government, economy, people, cultural life and society of traditional and modern Vietnam.
        Includes bibliographical references and index.
        ISBN: 0-8225-4678-7 (lib. bdg. : alk. paper)
        1. Vietnam. [1. Vietnam.] I. Title. II. Visual geography series (Minneapolis, Minn.)
DS556.3 .T38 2003
959.7—dc21   2002005524

Manufactured in the United States of America
1 2 3 4 5 6 - JR - 08 07 06 05 04 03

INTRODUCTION

Vietnam's people often compare the shape of their country to a *don ganh*, a long pole with rice baskets on each end. The Red River Delta in the north and the Mekong River Delta in the south are the "rice baskets," and the narrow coastal land running between them serves as the "pole."

Located in Southeast Asia, this mostly rural nation is home to nearly 79 million people. Since its first settlement thousands of years ago, Vietnam's people have struggled to maintain their identity and independence. While centuries of war and occupation have shaped the country's customs, the independent spirit of its people has kept the country's culture uniquely Vietnamese.

Knowing Vietnam's history is important to understanding the country itself. Since the first inhabitants settled the Red River Delta four thousand years ago, the struggle for independence has played a major role in shaping the country. The first of many foreign occupations occurred when China seized the area in 111 B.C. The Chinese ruled the country for one thousand years. During that time,

Chinese culture influenced the Vietnamese, but Vietnam's people retained their own language and culture and fought for self-rule in frequent rebellions.

When Vietnam won its independence from China in the tenth century A.D., the country expanded southward. By the mid-1700s, the Vietnam kingdom stretched from the Red River Delta in the north to the Mekong River Delta in the south. European merchants and traders discovered the fertile country around this same time. By the 1880s, the French had established separate colonies in southern, central, and northern Vietnam. Again the country found itself living under foreign rule.

After the end of World War II (1939–1945), Vietnamese nationalist and Communist organizations known as the Viet Minh proclaimed Vietnam's independence. France refused to give up its Southeast Asian colonies, however, and war broke out. Viet Minh guerrilla fighters defeated the French in 1954, and Vietnam declared its independence.

A postwar peace conference temporarily divided the nation into two parts—North Vietnam and South Vietnam. North Vietnam adopted Communism, an economic system in which the state owns and controls all farms, banks, and factories. South Vietnam allowed private ownership of property and supported a free-market system. In South Vietnam, supply and demand—not state controls—determined economic success or failure.

These differences led to civil war in the 1960s. Communist nations, such as the Soviet Union, backed North Vietnam. The United States and other free-market countries supported South Vietnam. Despite the presence of thousands of U.S. troops, North Vietnam gradually gained the upper hand with the use of guerrilla tactics. By 1973, U.S. forces had pulled out of South Vietnam, which soon fell to North Vietnam's forces. The two parts of the country reunited under Communist rule in 1976.

The reunification of Vietnam caused rejoicing as well as problems for the country. Badly damaged from the war, the country needed immediate investment to rebuild its farms, factories, power lines, and roads. The United States ended diplomatic relations with Vietnam and imposed a trade embargo, meaning the United States would neither buy goods from nor sell goods to Vietnam. Vietnam turned to the Soviet Union and other Communist countries for aid. To increase production and to bring the nation under one economic system, the Vietnamese government took over southern farms and businesses. It also set up programs to address the nation's economic problems.

By the late 1980s, however, it was clear that the government's plans were not working. Unemployment was rising, and consumer goods were still in short supply. New leaders saw the need for change and adopted *doi moi*, a package of economic reforms.

Doi moi allowed for some private ownership of land and businesses, while the government retained control over industry. In the early 1990s, Vietnam's economy was showing signs of recovery and growth. In major cities, small businesses sprang up, and foreign corporations opened offices.

The new millennium also ushered in new hope. In 2000 Vietnam began developing its computer industry in hopes of furthering the country's economic goals. Independent at last, Vietnam's people are working hard to create a bright future.

THE LAND

Vietnam stretches along the eastern edge of the Indochinese Peninsula in Southeast Asia. The country, which is shaped like a long capital *S*, covers 128,066 square miles (331,689 square kilometers), an area roughly equal to the size of New Mexico.

Vietnam's eastern and southern coasts meet the South China Sea. The Gulf of Tonkin lies off northeastern Vietnam. The southern tip of the country juts into the Gulf of Thailand, another arm of the South China Sea. China is Vietnam's northern neighbor. To the west are Cambodia and Laos.

In addition to its territory on the Asian continent, Vietnam claims ownership of several islands in the South China Sea, including the Paracels and Spratlys. These island groups, which China and Taiwan also claim, occupy areas of ocean that might hold large and valuable reserves of oil. Vietnamese historians claim that the islands belonged to the country during imperial times—before French occupation in the nineteenth century.

Topography

Vietnam's varied terrain includes flat, fertile cropland as well as rugged, forested mountains. The Red River and Mekong River Deltas together make up almost 25 percent of the country's area. A long, narrow strip of coastal lowland connects the two deltas. Hills and mountains, especially in the north and west, cover the rest of Vietnam.

Except for the lowlands of the Red River Delta, northern Vietnam is mountainous, with some ranges reaching more than 10,000 feet (3,048 meters) above sea level. Most of these highlands are forested, mainly with evergreens and valuable hardwoods. The country's tallest peak, Fan Si Pan, rises to 10,312 feet (3,143 m) near the Chinese border.

The Red River Delta has received deposits of waterborne silt for centuries. The fertile soil allows farmers in the region to harvest two, and sometimes three, rice crops each year. The Vietnamese have built more than 1,800 miles (2,897 km) of dikes, canals, and levees to prevent flooding in the region, but floods still cause damage.

Watery, segmented **rice paddies** dot Vietnam's landscape. Rice farming has been a major source of income for Vietnamese farmers for centuries.

Bordering the South China Sea are the sandy coastal lowlands, which in some places narrow to only 30 miles (48 km) across. Although not as heavily populated as either delta, the coastal lowlands support fishing and rice farming. Tourism is also important to the region's economy.

West of the coastal lowlands and south of the Red River Delta are the Truong Son Mountains, also called the Annamite Chain. The tallest parts of the range, which stretches westward into Laos, climb about 8,700 feet (2,652 m) above sea level. The Truong Son border a plateau region in central Vietnam called the Central Highlands. Inhabited by nomadic groups, the Central Highlands have fertile soil that nourishes tea plants and rubber trees.

Larger than the Red River Delta, the Mekong Delta is home to more than half the population of southern Vietnam and is the country's main farming area. The delta's rich soils, deposited by the Mekong and its feeder rivers, are especially suited to rice growing.

Rivers

The 500-mile-long (805 km) Red River begins in Yunnan, a southern province in China, and forms a 30-mile (48 km) section of the Vietnamese-Chinese border. The rapidly flowing waterway enters Vietnam northwest of the capital city of Hanoi and is eventually joined by the Lo River and the Da River. The Red River divides into branches that cross the delta and empty into the Gulf of Tonkin at five different locations.

During the 1960s and 1970s, the Ben Hai River served as the dividing line between North and South Vietnam. One small, rickety bridge spanned the river. The northern half was painted blue, and the southern half was painted green. Families, separated by the small bridge and the war, sometimes fought against each other.

The Mekong River starts its 2,600-mile (4,184 km) course in China and forms part of the borders of Myanmar (formerly Burma), Laos, and Thailand. As it enters Cambodia, the Mekong broadens and eventually divides into two main branches—the Lower River and the Upper River. After arriving in Vietnam, the Lower River flows directly into the South China Sea. The Upper River splits into six branches before reaching the sea. These rivers carry enormous amounts of fertile soil from the mountains to the delta lowland.

During the rainy season, the surging Mekong backs up into Tonle Sap, a large lake in Cambodia. This natural reservoir, with the help of an extensive canal system, reduces the danger of flooding and prevents the Mekong River Delta from drying out between rainy seasons.

Although the Red and Mekong Rivers dominate Vietnam's waterways, the country has dozens of smaller rivers. Most of these rise in the northern or western mountains and flow eastward toward the

Vietnam's rivers form the backbone of the country's transportation system. **The Red River** is one of the largest in the country. Take an online tour of the Red River Delta—go to vgsbooks.com.

South China Sea. One of these waterways—the Ben Hai River—once marked the boundary between North and South Vietnam.

Climate

Vietnam lies entirely within the tropics, an area of warm temperatures and little seasonal change. Nevertheless, the country's climate varies from south to north because of differences in terrain and altitude.

April and May are the hottest and most humid months in the south. In April the average temperature in Ho Chi Minh City (formerly Saigon) is 86°F (30°C). In December, the south's coldest month, the temperature averages 79°F (26°C).

The northern provinces have a cool season from December to March. In January, the north's coldest month, Hanoi's average daily reading is 62°F (17°C). In June, the warmest month, the average reading is 85°F (29°C).

Monsoons (seasonal, rain-bearing winds) determine Vietnam's patterns of rainfall. From May to November, monsoons sweep across southern Vietnam, the Central Highlands, and the northern mountains. These winds bring short, daily downpours. Winter monsoons, which arrive from the northeast between November and March, pick up moisture from the South China Sea. As the winds move inland, they dump rainfall on the northern half of Vietnam. Most parts of the country receive nearly 80 inches (203 centimeters) of annual precipitation, but some sections of the Central Highlands get 130 inches (330 cm).

Monsoon damage

In February and March, a persistent drizzle that the Vietnamese nickname "rain dust" falls in the north. Between July and November, violent storms called typhoons sometimes develop over the ocean and hit northern and central Vietnam with destructive force.

Flora and Fauna

Vietnam's warm, wet climate is ideal for the growth of many types of flowers and plants. Lush orchids thrive near the resort city of Da Lat, where florists ship the flowers to worldwide markets. Epiphytes—rootless plants that hang on trees—take their nourishment from particles in the air. The fingerlike shoots of lianas, a climbing vine, cling to the trunks of tropical trees.

Centuries ago, vast tropical forests of teak, mahogany, dipterocarps, and other hardwoods covered the highest elevations of Vietnam. At slightly lower levels, species of pine and other evergreens flourished. Mangrove trees, which local people cut and burned as cooking fuel, grew in swampy coastal regions. But only about one-third of these original forests remain.

The deforestation has resulted in part from increasing demands for farmland and wood by a growing population. In addition, many trees were lost during the Vietnam War of the 1960s and 1970s. To uncover the hideouts of opposing forces, U.S. planes destroyed huge areas of forested land through bombing or chemical spraying. For example, in 1968 the U Minh Forest in southern Vietnam burned for nearly seven weeks after being bombed, destroying 85 percent of its trees.

A national plan to reforest Vietnam began in the mid-1980s. Work crews planted 500 million trees, including nonnative eucalyptus and acacia that act as a protective umbrella for the more delicate native trees. In the shade of these species, foresters raise seedlings of bamboo, dipterocarps, and other valuable kinds of timber.

NEW SPECIES IN VIETNAM

Despite the loss of natural habitat, parts of Vietnam's wilderness remain virtually untouched by humans. Because of this, scientists are still finding and learning about new species of animals. In the Vu Quong Nature Reserve, the *saola*—a species of ox—was discovered by scientists in 1992. Also in the 1990s, scientists found two new species of muntjac (deer) in the same area. These finds have helped scientists and conservationists convince government officials to protect the biodiversity of the land.

The loss of forested land has deprived many animals of their habitats. The Javan rhinoceros and the *kouprey* (a forest ox), for example, have very limited ranges and are in danger of becoming extinct. The government has recognized 54 species of mammals and 60 species of birds as endangered. Yet Vietnam still contains more than 270 species of mammals, including elephants, tigers, leopards, black bears, serows (mountain goats), and bantengs (wild oxen). New laws that limit hunting help to protect these species. These laws also protect primates such as langurs, gibbons, and macaques.

Vietnam is home to 180 different kinds of reptiles, including crocodiles, pythons, and cobras. Amphibians and fish also thrive in the country's tropical climate. More than 700 bird species have been identified in Vietnam, especially in the deltas and along the coasts. Farmers raise partridges, ducks, and other birds as sources of food.

While conservation laws protect Vietnam's natural resources, limited funds and a lack of conservation officers make it difficult to enforce these laws. Vietnam's dwindling forests still provide hardwoods, particularly mahogany and teak, for the furniture and building industries. Illegal hunting of endangered animals, along with legal and illegal logging, continue to threaten the land.

Natural Resources

Northern Vietnam contains most of the country's natural resources. Large deposits of coal, a major source of fuel, are located near Hanoi. Factories in the port of Haiphong process some of the region's stocks of phosphates, a mineral used in making fertilizer. Other mineral resources include zinc, tin, manganese, and bauxite (the raw material for making aluminum).

Foreign contracts to tap offshore oil and gas reserves in the South China Sea have helped the country earn much-needed income. After refining, this oil also helps meet some of Vietnam's own energy demands.

The waters in and around Vietnam are a source of freshwater and saltwater seafood, chiefly shrimp, crab, lobster, mackerel, and tuna. Much of the catch is sold locally, but workers process some for export.

Cities

Twenty-four percent of Vietnam's 78.7 million people live in urban areas, the largest being Ho Chi Minh City (Saigon), Hanoi, and Haiphong. Important secondary cities include Da Nang, Nha Trang, and Hué, all of which lie along the coast of central Vietnam.

Saigon and its surrounding area in the Mekong Delta are home to 4.3 million people. The city's seldom-used official name—Ho Chi Minh City—honors the Communist leader who fought for Vietnam's independence from France.

HO CHI MINH CITY Founded in the sixth century A.D. by the Khmer of Cambodia, Ho Chi Minh City belonged to the Khmer Empire until the 1600s. At that time, the Vietnamese pushed southward and settled the lands around Ho Chi Minh City, which became a busy port. The port attracted the French, who seized the city in 1861 and made it a colonial capital. They constructed broad streets and European-style buildings in the city's neighborhoods, many of which still have a French look.

During the Vietnam War, thousands of U.S. troops, journalists, and civilians filled the hotels, nightclubs, and cafés of Ho Chi Minh City, whose economy was closely tied to wartime activity. After the war ended,

In **Ho Chi Minh City,** Vietnam's largest city, billboards advertise foreign and domestic products.

the city's economy slowed. Many businesses closed, and many others were seized by the government. Doi moi's economic improvements helped nightspots and restaurants to reopen, and construction contractors work hard to keep up with the demand for tourist lodging and office space. Souvenir shops and food vendors do a brisk business, and bicycles, cyclos (bicycle taxis), and motor scooters crowd the city's avenues.

The financial and commercial center of southern Vietnam, Ho Chi Minh City is still recovering from decades of war. The city's factories process food and make household items, including furniture and carpets. Small, family-owned businesses are flourishing, and outdoor food markets that once lacked goods display a wide variety of fruits and vegetables.

HANOI Some 3.7 million people live in the districts that make up greater Hanoi, Vietnam's second largest urban center. Four of the districts form the capital city of Hanoi, the industrial hub of northern Vietnam. Factories in the city manufacture building materials, chemicals, processed foods, electronics, and textiles. Economic reforms have encouraged foreign investments in Hanoi, and many private businesses have opened as a result.

Located along the Red River about 45 miles (72 km) inland from the Gulf of Tonkin, Hanoi began as the capital of the Ly dynasty (an early Vietnamese family of rulers) in A.D. 1010. The city continued to be an important cultural and educational center even after Emperor Gia Long moved the kingdom's capital to Hué in the 1800s.

In the heart of downtown Hanoi is Hoan Kiem Lake (Lake of the Restored Sword). In the surrounding park, Hanoi's residents hold festivals, bike races, and dove-flying competitions. South of the lake is a modern commercial section, where French-colonial buildings house hotels and large stores. North of Hoan Kiem Lake is Hanoi's old quarter, the site of ancient temples and of Ho Chi Minh's Mausoleum (aboveground tomb).

HAIPHONG Situated 65 miles (105 km) east of the capital on the Gulf of Tonkin, Haiphong (population 1.5 million) is the principal seaport of Hanoi and of northern Vietnam. Goods shipped into Haiphong go by rail to the capital. In the harbor, dozens of small boats compete for space with barges, tugboats, and cargo vessels.

Established by the French in the late 1800s, Haiphong came under Japanese rule in World War II. During the Vietnam War, most of North Vietnam's imported military supplies arrived in Haiphong. As a result, the port became the target of heavy U.S. bombing.

Haiphong's major industries produce ships, canned fish, glass, and textiles. A few plants process phosphates into farm fertilizers. Generating stations transfer electricity from nearby hydropower stations to Haiphong's factories. In keeping with the city's seafaring past, Haiphong is also the site of two institutes of oceanography and marine research.

SECONDARY CITIES Da Nang (population 382,674) sits midway along the country's eastern coast. The city's port facilities, which have been rebuilt since the 1970s, serve central Vietnam and landlocked Laos. During the Vietnam War, Da Nang's huge U.S.-built air base saw the arrival of many servicepeople, who relaxed at the local beaches when on leave. After the war, the resale of the base's military scrap metal helped revive the local economy.

Hué (population 219,149) is located 45 miles (72 km) north of Da Nang and 11 miles (18 km) inland from the coast. Established in 1802 by Emperor Gia Long, Hué was Vietnam's capital until 1945 and remains a cultural, religious, and educational center. The Citadel, a stronghold built by Gia Long, dominates the city from its site along the Perfume River.

Nha Trang (population 221,331) is an important fishing port on Vietnam's southeastern coast. A local fleet of about ten thousand small boats brings in lobster, shrimp, scallops, abalone, mackerel, and other varieties of seafood. The production of salt from nearby deposits employs thousands of the city's workers. Nha Trang also exports cash crops—such as latex from rubber trees and tea from tea plants—that are grown in the surrounding area.

HISTORY AND GOVERNMENT

The history of Vietnam begins in the Red River Delta, where the ancestors of the modern Vietnamese lived at least four thousand years ago. These people later moved southward in search of more farmland. In what became central Vietnam, they met the Cham—a people ethnically related to modern Cambodians—and the Khmer, who controlled the Mekong River Delta. Early contact with the Cham and the Khmer eventually resulted in conflict. By the mid-1700s A.D., the Vietnamese had defeated their rivals and were occupying all of the land that makes up modern Vietnam.

◉ Early Kingdoms

Excavations of ancient sites indicate that the first large, centrally organized state in the Red River Delta emerged around 800 B.C., a time known as the Dong-son period. The Dong-son people built dikes and canals to control the rivers of the delta. They used the tides of the South China Sea to irrigate their rice fields, which were called *lacs*.

By protecting the land from floods and droughts and by irrigating, the Dong-son produced dependable harvests.

Using small ships and canoes, the Dong-son people also traveled and traded. Through trading contacts on the Indochinese Peninsula, they expanded their knowledge of metalworking and learned to mold bronze into farm tools, weapons, and drums.

Around 500 B.C., the Sa Hyunh culture from present-day Borneo moved into southern Vietnam. Their pottery and jewelry techniques were adopted by the people living in the Mekong Delta.

Around 300 B.C., people in the region were divided into the Tay Au and the Lac Viet. Little is known about these groups except that the Tay Au lived in the highlands and the Lac Viet lived on the plains.

By 250 B.C., a Vietnamese ruler named An Duong Vuong had created the Au Lac kingdom by bringing together the people living in the delta and the peoples of the neighboring highlands. The Au Lac capital, at Co Loa, was 20 miles (32 km) north of present-day Hanoi.

Most of the kingdom's people were rice farmers who worked the lacs that belonged to local nobles.

Zhao Tuo, a Chinese commander, conquered the Red River Delta in 207 B.C. and set up Nam Viet, an independent kingdom. (In Chinese, *nam* means "south" and *Viet* refers to the peoples living along China's southern frontier.) In 111 B.C., a wave of Chinese imperial armies seized Nam Viet and made it a Chinese province.

China's culture helped shape Vietnamese society. The Chinese philosophy of Confucianism, for example, provided Vietnam with a strict system for governing and for daily life. The Vietnamese also adopted the Chinese picture-characters that Confucian officials and educators used for reading and writing.

Some Vietnamese nobles—including two sisters, Trung Trac and Trung Nhi—resisted Chinese ways. The sisters led a rebellion in A.D. 39 that restored Nam Viet's independence. But most of the local aristocracy failed to support the Trung sisters, and China's overwhelming power helped it regain control in 43.

Chinese rule of Vietnam lasted one thousand years. During that time, educated Vietnamese accepted some aspects of Chinese culture, including the Chinese form of the Buddhist faith. The Chinese also taught Vietnamese workers to breed silkworms, mint coins, and manufacture porcelain. Along Vietnam's coasts, the Chinese constructed several harbors to foster international trade. Some Vietnamese families acquired wealth and power as trade increased.

China's rule was not uncontested, however. The independent kingdom of Cham emerged in central Vietnam in 192, when a local official overthrew the Chinese authority in the region. The Cham Empire extended west from Hué into what later became Cambodia and Laos. The Chams fought with China and later with the Vietnamese empire over its territory.

THE TRUNG SISTERS

After the Chinese executed her husband for treason, Trung Trac raised troops and—with the help of her sister, Trung Nhi—pushed the Chinese out of Nam Viet. Three years later, the Chinese crushed the revolt, and the sisters threw themselves into a river.

While their liberation was short lived, the memory of the sisters was not. The Vietnamese eventually built pagodas (temples) to honor them and used their bravery as an inspiration for later rebellions. The government proclaimed them national heroes, and Vietnamese girls honor their memory on Hai Ba Trung Day in March. Visit vgsbooks.com for links where you can learn more about the Trung sisters.

The **lavish architecture** of the Cham Empire was influenced by the early Indian Empire.

By 200 the Chinese Han dynasty had retaken control of the empire, and Vietnam's name was changed to Giao Chau. Another empire at this time, India, also began to influence people in the region. During the fourth and fifth centuries, trade with India flourished.

China's Han dynasty fell in the mid-500s, and the Chams attacked Vietnam in 543. Chinese general Pham Tu defeated the Chams and renamed the area Van Xuan. During this time, peoples in the area were exposed to Indian political and religious ideas, such as Buddhism and Hinduism.

In 679, under the rule of China's Tang dynasty, the country was again renamed. This time the area was called Annam, or "pacified south."

By 700 central Vietnam had become a major power center for the Cham Empire. During this time, many Cham buildings were constructed, including the temple complex at My Son.

In the mid-800s, the Thais, an ethnic group from China, attacked and held Vietnam for three years. China's rulers were able to oust the Thais, but the attacks had exposed the weakness of the ruling Chinese elite.

Independence and Conquest

In the tenth century, political upheaval in China gave the Vietnamese a chance to challenge Chinese rule. Led by Ngo Quyen, a rebel army defeated the Chinese and declared Vietnam's independence in 939. Ngo set up a capital at Co Loa but did not live long enough to create a strong state. After Ngo's death in 944, the region's wealthy landowning families competed for power.

Ly Thai Tho built the **Temple of Literature (Van Mieu)** in 1070 for Confucian scholars to use. The temple is located in modern-day Hanoi.

In 1009 Ly Thai Tho, the head of one of these families, seized control and later founded the capital of his Ly dynasty on the site of modern Hanoi. The country—which was renamed Dai Viet (Great Viet)—developed an effective central government that was organized according to Confucian ideas. Confucian scholars had to train for years and then pass tough civil-service examinations before joining the mandarins, an elite group of bureaucrats that ran the government.

During the Ly reign, the Vietnamese began to move southward in search of new fields. In central Vietnam lay the unplanted lands of the Chams. Vietnamese armies attacked the Cham kingdom and forced the Cham ruler to give up some of his provinces. Vietnamese farmers began to cultivate rice in the coastal lowlands, where engineers built dikes and canals to control flooding.

Also during the Ly dynasty, Buddhism was adopted as Vietnam's official religion. But many people also incorporated the spirit worship of their ancestors into the Buddhist faith.

The Ly dynasty lasted until 1225, when the Tran family came to power. Tran rulers further improved the country's administration and economy. Water-control projects allowed farmers to plant more crops and to produce bigger harvests, which led to economic prosperity. Mandarins continued to guide the country, and the Buddhist religion continued to flourish.

In 1257 and 1284, Mongol armies from eastern Asia attacked Dai Viet, briefly taking over the capital both times. In 1288 General Tran Hung Dao led the Viet army against a third invasion and defeated the Mongol threat for the final time.

Throughout the 1300s, Tran armies also fought with Cham over the provinces it still had in central Vietnam. Seeking help, Cham's ruler asked the Chinese to attack the Vietnamese kingdom. China agreed and, as a result, by 1407 Dai Viet had lost its independence to the Chinese Empire.

The Chinese emperor required local nobles to wear Chinese clothing and banned the teaching of the Vietnamese language. China's harsh rule soon stirred revolts in Vietnam. Le Loi, a wealthy landowner, organized a resistance movement that expelled the Chinese in 1427. He set up the Le dynasty, whose capital was in present-day Hanoi.

Under the Le kings, Dai Viet enjoyed political stability. Le Thanh Tong, one of the greatest of the Le rulers, established a new legal system and ordered the writing of a fifteen-volume history of Dai Viet. He also expanded Vietnam's territory southward by completely annexing (taking over) Cham in 1471.

Division and Unity

After Le Thanh Tong's death in 1497, weak Le rulers ignored the well-organized Confucian system of governing, and the central government fell apart. In the early 1500s, strong clans (family groups) fought one another for power. In 1527 Mac Dang Dung, the head of one clan, overthrew the Le rulers, and a long civil war broke out.

By the late sixteenth century, two families dominated the country. The Trinh family, the real power in the north, reinstated the weak Le monarchs to serve as figurehead rulers (rulers in name only). The south was ruled by the Nguyen family, which was using its army to annex land belonging to the Khmer Empire. The Khmers controlled a broad section of the Indochinese Peninsula, including the fertile Mekong Delta.

By 1690 the Nguyen family had succeeded and had taken over Saigon, a Khmer settlement within the Mekong Delta. The Nguyen family also increased its international trade links by supplying silks and precious metals to Chinese, Japanese, and European merchants. Farmers on Nguyen plantations grew sugarcane and other crops for world markets. Meanwhile, European traders, accompanied by Roman Catholic missionaries, worked hard to build trade and to win Vietnamese converts to Christianity.

Despite the expanding power of the Nguyen family, the Vietnamese who settled in the Mekong Delta wanted to be independent. In 1771 three brothers led a rebellion from Tay Son, a village located in eastern Vietnam. In the 1780s, after several years of fighting, the Tay Son army drove Nguyen forces from the Mekong Delta and then defeated the Trinh army in the north.

After taking over northern, central, and southern Vietnam, the brothers tried to set up a unified government. The Tay Son regime, however, could not solve the problems caused by years of war, such as damaged farms, poor harvests, and famine.

In nearby Thailand, a young survivor of the Nguyen clan, Nguyen Anh, planned to regain Vietnam. He got the backing of France and other foreign powers, which were setting up commercial outposts in Asia. Nguyen Anh's forces marched northward from the Mekong Delta and finally defeated the Tay Son army in 1802. After his forces overran most of present-day Vietnam, Nguyen Anh founded the Nguyen imperial dynasty and named himself Emperor Gia Long.

In the 1820s and 1830s, Gia Long's son and successor, Minh Mang, disliked French influence. Even after the emperor executed dozens of French missionaries, some missionaries and merchants continued to work in Vietnam and to call for a French takeover of the region.

This tomb was built for Minh Mang, son of Emperor Gia Long.

French Control

French merchants of the 1840s were eager to exploit Vietnam's economic resources. They pressured the French emperor, Napoleon III, to invade. A French fleet successfully attacked Da Nang in 1858 but was unable to hold on to the port. After the French captured Saigon the next year, they forced the Nguyen ruler to give up the Mekong Delta. By 1867 France had established the southern region as the French colony of Cochin China.

French troops advanced farther north in the early 1880s, attacking Hué and the Red River Delta. By the end of the decade, central Vietnam (called Annam) and northern Vietnam (called Tonkin) were in French hands. France combined these two regions with Cochin China, Cambodia, and Laos—which France also controlled—to form the Union of Indochina. A French-appointed governor-general oversaw the union, while the Nguyen monarch became the figurehead ruler. The French set up schools to teach the children of wealthy Vietnamese. These schools encouraged the development of Vietnamese scholars and intellectuals.

Colonial administrators developed and exploited Vietnam's natural resources. To expand rice production in the Mekong Delta, the French drained swamps and built irrigation systems. The colonial government gave land along the Cambodian border to French settlers, who established large farms and rubber plantations. Landowners in the sparsely populated Central Highlands cultivated tea and other cash crops for export. In the north, the French mined coal and minerals. These efforts created very different economies in the north and south. The north became largely industrial, while the south continued to be mainly agricultural.

The French used Vietnamese laborers to build ports, roads, bridges, and railway lines to ship goods to market. Most of the economic development of Vietnam did not benefit the local people, however. Most farmers worked for landowners who did not live on the farms they owned. These absentee landlords exported the crops instead of selling them locally. Having lost their land, many Vietnamese had to find work in coal mines or on rubber plantations, where the pay was low and the working conditions were hard.

Resistance Movements and World War II

The harshness of French colonial rule strengthened Vietnamese opposition to the Union of Indochina. Poor farmers protested high taxes, government corruption, and the growing power of absentee landowners. In the early twentieth century, a group of Vietnamese scholars set up an association that sought to overthrow French rule and to establish a constitutional government.

In the 1920s, the Communist philosophy of Vladimir Lenin, the leader of the Soviet Union, inspired a new generation of nationalists, including a young activist named Ho Chi Minh. Communists favored state ownership of all property, including farms, factories, and mines. During a stay in France, Ho became active in the French Communist Party, which encouraged him to organize a Communist movement in his homeland. By 1930 Ho had formed the Indochinese Communist Party (ICP).

During the worldwide economic depression of the 1930s, the Vietnamese struggled to survive, and political unrest largely ceased. The ICP used this peaceful time to broaden its support among farmers, factory workers, and managers. The party was especially successful in Annam and Tonkin, where the depression was causing much anti-French feeling. By the end of the 1930s, a number of nationalist, non-Communist parties also existed in Vietnam. They and the ICP strongly opposed French colonial power.

Ho Chi Minh (shown here in the 1930s), became a major figure in twentieth-century Vietnamese politics. He began his career as a Communist activist. To find additional information about Ho Chi Minh, go to vgsbooks.com.

In 1940 France was occupied by German forces during World War II. France agreed to a treaty allowing Japan to station troops in its Indochina colony. In exchange for the right to use Vietnam's military facilities and to station troops in Vietnam, the Japanese allowed the French to remain in charge of the Union of Indochina. Japanese forces soon occupied all Indochina.

The leaders of many nationalist parties, including the ICP, retreated to southern China where they formed a united front to oppose Japan and to win Vietnam's independence. This organization—called the Viet Minh, or League of Independence of Vietnam—prepared its members to stage a postwar revolt against the French and to throw out the Nguyen monarch.

VIETNAMESE DYNASTIES	
Ngo	A.D. 939–965
Dinh	968–980
Early Le	980–1009
Ly	1009–1225
Tran	1225–1400
Ho	1400–1407
Later Le	1428–1789
Nguyen and Trinh lords	1592–1788
Tay Son	1788–1802
Nguyen	1802–1945

The First Indochina War

On August 12, 1945, Japan surrendered to Britain and the United States, and World War II ended. Within days the Viet Minh set up a temporary government in Hanoi headed by Ho Chi Minh, who formed the independent Democratic Republic of Vietnam (DRV). Although strong in Tonkin and Annam, the Viet Minh did not have as much support in Cochin China. French officials and the DRV could not agree on how to govern Vietnam. Tensions grew, and in December 1946, war broke out.

For the next eight years, fighting raged between the Viet Minh and the French—a conflict the Vietnamese call the First Indochina War. The French used superior weapons to seize strategic airfields and cities. The Viet Minh, on the other hand, trained guerrillas (small bands of rebel fighters) to attack French outposts in the countryside. In May 1954, the Viet Minh defeated the French at Dien Bien Phu, a town in northwestern Vietnam. As a result, France decided to settle for peace. At a conference in Geneva, Switzerland, France agreed to the independence of all its Indochinese colonies.

The country needed to decide on its new leadership. Until then, the conference temporarily divided Vietnam into two zones along the Ben Hai River. North Vietnam remained under the control of the DRV and was led by the party's general secretary, Ho Chi Minh. Bao Dai, the last Nguyen monarch, became head of the government of the Associated State of Vietnam, also called South Vietnam.

The peace agreement instructed both governments to cease hostilities and to prepare for national elections that would reunify Vietnam. Although Bao Dai supported the cease-fire, he did not back the elections. DRV officials, who thought the southern government was weak and would quickly fall, supported national elections to begin reunification.

Two Vietnams

Bao Dai's prime minister, Ngo Dinh Diem, used harsh measures to stabilize the South Vietnamese government. Diem's growing power made him a strong rival for the country's leadership. In October 1955, he defeated Bao Dai in a public vote in the south and proclaimed himself president of the newly named Republic of Vietnam.

Though he was popular at first, Diem lost support through greed and corruption. He used his political power to increase his own and his family's wealth. A staunch Roman Catholic, Diem also persecuted members of the Buddhist clergy and ordered government troops to raid several Buddhist temples.

Ngo Dinh Diem

At the same time, North Vietnam's government began to wage guerrilla warfare in South Vietnam. The DRV supported and trained the growing forces of the National Liberation Front (NLF). Also called the Viet Cong, this mobile group of guerrilla fighters sought reunification of the country under the DRV's Communist regime.

By the early 1960s, the conflict in Vietnam—locally known as the Second Indochina War—had begun to gain international attention. Many countries, including the United States and the Soviet Union, viewed the war as an important regional struggle between the forces of democracy and Communism.

The U.S. government, headed by President John F. Kennedy, feared that Communist control of Vietnam would open the door for a Communist takeover of all of Southeast Asia. To prevent that outcome, the Kennedy administration decided to give military aid to South Vietnam. Meanwhile, the United States disapproved of Diem's harsh government. Encouraged by U.S. officials, anti-Diem military officers overthrew Diem in November 1963. A military junta (ruling group) took over the government of South Vietnam.

Sensing a chance to weaken the new regime and to attract more southern support, North Vietnam and the NLF sent additional guerrilla forces into the south. Many of the units used the Ho Chi Minh Trail, a network of jungle paths that passed from North Vietnam through Laos and Cambodia to South Vietnam. Money, weapons, and training from Communist nations such as China and the Soviet Union helped the North Vietnamese and the NLF to harass South Vietnam's troops.

In August 1964, a North Vietnamese gunboat attacked a U.S. ship patrolling the Gulf of Tonkin. The United States responded by increasing its own involvement in Vietnam. In 1965 President Lyndon B. Johnson, who had succeeded Kennedy, authorized air strikes against North Vietnam and sent the first U.S. combat troops into South Vietnam.

War and Withdrawal

Between 1965 and 1968, the Vietnam War was at its height. Neither side won decisive victories, and each used different fighting tactics. North Vietnam specialized in guerrilla warfare, while South Vietnam, backed by U.S. troops, used superior weapons to stage major offensives. The United States heavily bombed Hanoi and Haiphong.

From the 1960s to the early 1970s, U.S. troops were stationed in Vietnam.

THE CU CHI TUNNELS

The villages around Cu Chi in South Vietnam supported the Viet Cong during the Vietnam War. To hide from American soldiers, the Viet Cong dug their way out of harm's way—creating the legendary Cu Chi Tunnels. By 1965 the Viet Cong had 120 miles (193 km) of tunnels under the area, making it possible for guerrillas to attack and quickly disappear again.

Because the guerrillas lived in the tunnels for weeks, or even months, tunnel complexes included bathrooms, meeting rooms, kitchens, and dorms. But life in the tunnels was harsh. American soldiers repeatedly attempted to flush out the tunnels, and tunnel dwellers also dealt with scorpions, rats, and snakes. It is estimated that twelve thousand Vietnamese guerrillas perished in the tunnels during the war.

During the Tet Offensive in 1968, North Vietnam made an all-out effort to capture towns and villages in South Vietnam. (Tet, the Vietnamese New Year celebration, is an important national holiday. The attack broke a holiday truce.) North Vietnam believed the people in the countryside of South Vietnam would support the attack. Instead, North Vietnamese forces encountered strong resistance. The fighting became the worst of the war. After a month of intense combat, the death toll was 40,000 for North Vietnam; 2,300 for the United States; and 1,100 for South Vietnam.

Despite losses nearly twenty times more than its opposition, North Vietnam was determined to win the war. The increasing cost in troops and supplies caused the U.S. government to reconsider its role. The Johnson administration started talking about withdrawing from a conflict that was becoming hard to win in Vietnam and was increasingly unpopular in the United States.

Richard M. Nixon, who succeeded Johnson in 1969, announced a gradual withdrawal of U.S. troops from Vietnam. At the same time, South Vietnam's armed forces would continue to receive U.S. training and weapons. Nixon also renewed international efforts to negotiate peace between the warring sides.

U.S. bombing of North Vietnam went on, destroying cities, industries, power plants, and roads. After the death of Ho Chi Minh in 1969 and after several more years of fighting, North Vietnam agreed to attend peace talks, which resulted in the Paris Agreement of January 27, 1973. The last U.S. troops left Vietnam two months later.

Despite the agreement, there was little break in the fighting for the people of Vietnam. In 1974 South Vietnam's government declared a renewal of the war. North Vietnam responded by launching a major offensive in early 1975. Without the support of U.S. troops, South Vietnam's forces collapsed, and North Vietnam achieved a total victory at the end of April. Within a year, the two parts of Vietnam— at war since 1945 and split since 1954—were united into the Socialist Republic of Vietnam.

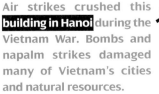

Visit vgsbooks.com to find a variety of resources on the Vietnam War—including additional information on the U.S. involvement, photographs of the fighting, stories from individuals directly involved or affected by the conflict, and more.

Challenges of Reunification

The new nation faced severe challenges. Many parts of the country were in ruins. Battles and bombings had destroyed farmland, industries, and roads. Because the Socialist Republic of Vietnam was a Communist nation, the United States broke diplomatic relations with Vietnam and banned U.S. companies from trading and investing there.

These problems were in the hands of Le Duan, who had succeeded Ho Chi Minh as general secretary (leader) of the Vietnamese

Air strikes crushed this **building in Hanoi** during the Vietnam War. Bombs and napalm strikes damaged many of Vietnam's cities and natural resources.

Communist Party. Duan made efforts to extend Vietnam's authority in Southeast Asia. In 1978 the country invaded Cambodia and installed a pro-Vietnamese regime. The Vietnamese also supported a Communist takeover in Laos.

These actions angered Chinese officials, who did not want Vietnam to dominate Indochina. China invaded northern Vietnam in 1979 and cut off Chinese aid and imports. Moreover, to show its disapproval of Vietnam's invasion of Cambodia, the United States strengthened its trade embargo (ban) by launching a campaign to stop diplomatic relations between Vietnam and international organizations such as the Association of Southeast Asian Nations (ASEAN). As a result of tighter economic restrictions, the nation drew closer to the Soviet Union, which became Vietnam's chief financial backer.

Despite Soviet support, Vietnam's economy continued to decline. Reunification had not solved the country's economic problems, nor had it eliminated the distinctions between the north and the south. The north was primarily an industrial center with an economy based on its plentiful energy resources and port facilities. The south was mainly agricultural, relying on productive farms and fertile soil. Both sections of the country were in need of immediate investment and modernization.

After the war, the government sought to unify the economies of the north and the south under a Communist system. Vietnamese officials collectivized southern farmland by combining small farms into large estates. The authorities also took over southern businesses, ending years of private ownership of industries. These actions put land and factories in the hands of the state, which employed workers and set production targets for farms and industries.

Economic Stress and Change

Throughout the late 1970s and early 1980s, the Vietnamese government was determined to implement its economic plans, by force if necessary. Officials uprooted segments of the population of crowded southern cities—mainly Saigon, which had been renamed Ho Chi Minh City—and resettled them in new economic zones (NEZs). In these rural zones, little industrial or agricultural development had ever taken place.

The government used the NEZs not only to relieve urban crowding but also to break up South Vietnam's social structure. Communist authorities sent many southern intellectuals and professionals to reeducation camps. At these rural stations, southerners were both coerced through forced labor and encouraged through study to accept the

Communist system. As a result of these harsh measures, thousands of people—many of them managers and skilled workers—fled the country in small boats, risking their lives for the chance to find a safer home and a better life.

> The boat people faced many dangers, including typhoons, starvation, disease, and pirates, in their search for safe harbor. Over the roughly fifteen years that the exodus continued, nearly 850,000 boat people survived to find asylum in new homes.

Despite its bold attempts to restructure the economy, the government of Vietnam failed to provide enough supplies of food and basic consumer goods. As the economy worsened, the inflation rate reached more than 700 percent a year. In the early 1980s, the politicians who controlled the Vietnamese Communist Party disagreed about how to achieve future goals. A conservative faction still pushed for centralized planning and public ownership of all farms and businesses. A liberal, reformist wing of the party thought that the government should change its strict economic policies.

Le Duan compromised to keep the party from splitting up over these differences. But after he died in July 1986, disputes erupted in the government. Eventually, Nguyen Van Linh, a reformist, became general secretary. He chose to work alongside Vo Van Kiet and Do Muoi, economic reformers in the Communist Party.

Old Problems and New Hope

In 1986 Linh, Muoi, and Kiet introduced doi moi (meaning "renovation"), a package of economic reforms that allowed some private ownership of businesses. The policy also granted long-term leases to farmers so they would be encouraged to develop their land. The new leaders devalued the Vietnamese currency, the dong, to bring down the soaring inflation rate. They also sought more financial aid from the Soviet Union and the Communist nations of Eastern Europe, which frequently traded and set up joint projects with Vietnam.

The attempts at reform improved the country's international standing. In 1989 Vietnam agreed to negotiate a settlement with Cambodia, and in 1991 the two countries signed a peace agreement that led to the withdrawal of Vietnamese troops. The following year, China began to mend its differences with Vietnam and gave its neighbor a small amount of economic aid. Vietnam's withdrawal from Cambodia gained the country an invitation to join ASEAN in 1995. Vietnam's economy immediately benefited from increased trade with other ASEAN nations, such as Thailand, Singapore, and Malaysia.

Communist propaganda, such as this billboard, was used to boost Vietnam's faith in the party during the 1990s.

In the early 1990s, growing political opposition and failing economies shook the Communist world. Many Eastern European nations toppled their Communist governments, and the Soviet Union broke up. In Vietnam, imports of oil, fertilizers, and raw materials from the former Soviet Union dropped sharply. Meanwhile, the continuing U.S. embargo slowed international investments in Vietnam and limited the country's trade with Japan and Europe. Despite these obstacles, Vietnamese leaders went ahead with their economic reform plans.

In 1991 Do Muoi succeeded Linh as general secretary of the Communist Party, and Kiet became prime minister. They continued their efforts to forge closer ties with the non-Communist world, while keeping tight control over domestic politics. By early 1994, the United States had lifted its trade embargo. The change was partly because Vietnam was helping to locate the remains of missing U.S. soldiers who had served in Vietnam.

International banks, with U.S. approval, began lending money to Vietnam. This move encouraged Asian nations, such as South Korea, Japan, Hong Kong, and Taiwan, to set up businesses in Vietnam. Europeans and Americans also opened factories in the country.

In 1995 the United States and Vietnam reestablished diplomatic ties by opening liaison offices in each other's capitals. The two nations slowly began working out details for a trade agreement. In exchange for full trading privileges, Vietnam agreed to pay compensation for U.S. property confiscated during the war. That same year, the Vietnamese government adopted its first-ever civil code, which gave people more opportunity to own land and property, to run private businesses, and to raise capital.

Several factors continued to hinder economic growth, however. Vietnam lacked a well-run banking system, which international investors needed for their operations. The continuing influence of the country's conservative bureaucrats also hindered progress.

The new millennium brought turbulence to the nation. In 2000 the Mekong River covered central Vietnam with the worst flood in forty years. More than 500 people died, and more than 750,000 people were left homeless. In 2001 ethnic violence broke out in the Central Highlands as Montagnards (mountain clans) attacked state offices and blocked roads to protest the migration of ethnic Vietnamese from urban areas.

But the new millennium also ushered in renewed hope. In 2001 the Central Committee of the Communist Party appointed Nong Duc Manh as general secretary. Manh, a moderate, hopes to further modernize the economy by developing industry.

As Vietnam works toward its economic and diplomatic goals, many of the nation's people are hopeful. The country's leadership, though resistant to political change, is eager for Vietnam to take its place among the thriving economies of Southeast Asia. The nation is making slow but steady progress toward a better future.

In 2001 **Nong Duc Manh** was appointed general secretary of the Vietnamese Communist Party, which runs the country.

◑ Government

Vietnam's government functions alongside the Communist Party, whose most powerful institution is the Political Bureau. The dozen or more high-level leaders of the Political Bureau issue directives to the government. Every four to six years, the roughly 2.4 million members of the Communist Party attend meetings, where major policies are discussed and set. The general secretary is the party's top administrator.

Vietnam's highest legislative body is the National Assembly, which has 450 deputies who serve five-year terms. Members of the National Assembly are elected by the Vietnamese people, and this legislative body, in turn, elects the president and the vice president. The assembly sets policy for the country's social and economic development, national financial plans, and foreign policy. The assembly chooses a council of ministers, which heads the various administrative departments and passes legislation.

Members of Vietnam's **National Assembly,** a 450-person legislative body, serve five-year terms. This group is responsible for electing the country's president.

The president is the head of state and runs the country's domestic and foreign affairs. With the backing of the National Assembly, the president appoints or dismisses members of government and declares war or a state of emergency. The president appoints the prime minister to run the day-to-day operations of government. Both the president and the prime minister serve for five years.

The Communist Party runs Vietnam's judicial system, whose highest tribunal is the Supreme People's Court. This court hears serious national cases, such as those for treason, and is the last court of appeals. People's courts operate at the provincial, district, and city levels. Although judges at each division can send a case to a higher court, most make final rulings at their own levels.

Vietnam is divided into fifty-eight provinces and the three independent city provinces of Hanoi, Ho Chi Minh City, and Haiphong. The elected provincial councils enjoy considerable independence from the central government.

THE PEOPLE

Most of Vietnam's 78.7 million people live in the lowlands of the Red River and Mekong River Deltas. The country's highest population density is in the Red River Delta, which holds more than 2,859 people per square mile (1,104 per sq. km). In Hanoi the population density reaches 6,063 people per square mile (2,341 per sq. km). The Mekong Delta has a lower density but a larger total population.

Vietnam's population is growing at an annual rate of 1.4 percent, a pace that will double the country's population by 2050. The Vietnamese government is working to slow population growth through family-planning programs. Birth control supplies are available to about 75 percent of all married couples. However, many couples continue to marry young and to have two or three children.

Even though 76 percent of the Vietnamese dwell in rural areas, there is much urban crowding. To relieve it, a government resettlement program has moved more than 10 million people to NEZs in the Central Highlands, in the coastal lowlands, and on nearby islands.

Most rural families live in thatched dwellings and work on state-owned or private farms. Small gardens supply the families with additional food. Few rural areas have electricity or public water supplies, and most families must carry water from nearby streams. These conditions give couples more reasons to have several children, who can share the work of farming the land and maintaining the home.

Most city dwellers live in small apartments, many of which house three generations of a single family. Furniture is sparse in most homes, and at mealtimes families traditionally sit on the floor around a small table. Wood, thatch, and bamboo are popular building materials for homes in the south, where the weather is warm year round. In the north, houses of stone protect residents from cooler temperatures and seasonal storms.

Ethnic Mixture

Nearly 90 percent of Vietnam's citizens are ethnic Vietnamese who are descendants of the early peoples of the Red River Delta. Ethnic

Even before the country's division in the twentieth century, northern and southern Vietnamese had their own unique characteristics and personalities. Northerners are often thought of as more conservative, with a strong sense of history. Southerners are considered more open to new ideas and strive to be more modern.

Vietnamese dominate the nation's administration and industry. Most senior officials of the Communist Party and of the government come from this group. Ethnic Vietnamese also hold most of the country's managerial jobs.

One reminder of the U.S. presence in southern Vietnam is the many Amerasians in Ho Chi Minh City. These people, the offspring of U.S. soldiers and ethnic Vietnamese women, have not been accepted into Vietnamese society and often live on the streets.

National Minorities

About 12 percent of Vietnam's population belong to fifty-four other ethnic groups, officially called national minorities. Most have their historic origins in Southeast Asia or southern China. Many live in remote areas that have been the last to receive educational and health benefits.

In the mountains of northern Vietnam, the largest ethnic groups are the Tay (1.2 million), the Muong (1 million), the Thai (1 million), the Hmong Meo (500,000), and the Zao (470,000). Thai speech is similar to the language spoken in Thailand, while the Muong language is closely related to Vietnamese. People from the Hmong Meo and Zao groups speak Sino-Tibetan dialects that are rooted in China.

Numerous ethnic communities, whom the French collectively called Montagnards (mountain people) populate the Central Highlands. These groups total about 1 million people and are very diverse in languages, customs, and appearance.

The Hmong Meo people are one of many minority groups living in modern Vietnam. The word *hmong* means "free."

This group of **Montagnards,** members of the Bru ethnic community, inhabit the mountainous regions of southern Vietnam near Khe Sanh.

The most numerous are the Jarai (200,000), the Ede (200,000), and the Bahnar (140,000). The majority of Montagnards are nomadic farmers. Some Montagnard groups have earned a reputation for skill in battle and were recruited to fight against North Vietnam during the war.

Also living in the Central Highlands are about 90,000 Chams, whose kingdom of Cham dominated central Vietnam until the late 1400s. After the Chams retreated to the highlands, they converted to the Islamic faith. Their culture was also greatly influenced by India and its Hindu beliefs, which many Chams still honor.

In southern Vietnam, the largest ethnic minority is the Khmer, who number about 1 million. The main ethnic group in Cambodia, the Khmer are closely related to the Mon people of Myanmar. The Khmer Empire once extended across the southern part of Southeast Asia and included all of the Mekong Delta. Most Vietnamese Khmer live west of Ho Chi Minh City and south of the Mekong Delta.

About 1 million ethnic Chinese, called Hoa, also live in the lowlands of southern Vietnam. In the early twentieth century, the Chinese dominated trade and banking, but many Vietnamese distrusted them. After the Communists reunified the nation, Vietnam's Chinese population became the target of persecution. As a result, thousands of Hoa fled to China in small boats, and many died before reaching their destinations.

Language

Vietnam's language reflects the complex history of its people. Most of the words used in everyday speech are identical to words in Mon-Khmer, the language spoken in Cambodia. Other Vietnamese words come from the Thai language. Many administrative, technical, and literary terms in Vietnamese are of Chinese origin.

This billboard uses the *quoc ngu* alphabet, which contains the same characters as English but which has markings, called diacritics, to aid in pronunciation.

For centuries Vietnamese scholars used the Chinese language and writing system. Later they developed *chu nom,* a form of writing that adapted Chinese ideograms (pictorial forms) to express Vietnamese words. Chu nom was used by scholars and the ruling class and was never widespread among the people.

The use of ideograms declined after the 1600s, when a Catholic missionary developed *quoc ngu,* an alphabet that employs Latin letters and that shows pronunciation with accent marks called diacritics. Writers and politicians continued to use chu nom, however, and Vietnamese authors wrote in chu nom until the colonial era. In the early 1900s, the French encouraged the use of quoc ngu, which allowed for better communication between French and Vietnamese officials. After 1945 quoc ngu became widely used in schools and literature.

Education

The Vietnamese have long valued education as a means to get better jobs and a higher rank in society. For centuries, however, education was available to only the richest Vietnamese families. Since the 1950s, schooling has been available to everyone, and attendance at public schools has been high. By 1998 nearly 10.5 million students were enrolled in primary schools. Although Vietnam does not have enough teachers, books, and school buildings, the country's literacy rate has risen to 93 percent.

French colonial officials introduced a European educational system, in which children begin primary school at the age of six. After five years, students enter secondary school, a four-year education that includes history, geography, literature, and sciences. In the 1990s, about 45 percent of primary-school graduates went on to secondary school. Students who do not attend secondary school can continue their education with technical or vocational training.

Ho Chi Minh City classroom

Students who do complete secondary school may choose to go on to one of the country's 104 colleges. The largest universities are in Hué, Hanoi, and Ho Chi Minh City.

Health

Decades of war and periodic famines have taken a toll on the health of the Vietnamese, and improving health care is a national priority. The government trains medical personnel, administers hospitals, distributes medicines, and coordinates medical research.

The Vietnamese receive free medical care, and almost every village has a health center staffed by part-time health workers. Patients who need more specialized treatment can go to district or urban health facilities. Shortages of drugs and medical equipment, however, limit the effectiveness of some types of treatment.

The infant mortality rate—the number of babies who die within their first year—is 37 in every 1,000 live births. This figure is lower than the average number for Southeast Asia and has been improving for several years. Life expectancy at birth is 66 years, which is also better than average for the region.

Among the diseases that still afflict the Vietnamese are bubonic plague and cholera. Doctors have made progress in controlling tuberculosis, typhoid, malaria, and trachoma. Despite government efforts to improve public health, widespread malnutrition makes the population susceptible to illness. In recent years, tens of thousands of Vietnamese babies have been born with birth defects. These defects may be linked to chemicals sprayed on forested areas during the Vietnam War.

MARRIAGE

In Vietnam, marriage is one of the most important events in a young person's life. In the past, families arranged marriages with the help of professional matchmakers and fortune-tellers. They ensured that the couple's horoscopes were compatible. While modern marriages are no longer arranged, the ceremonies still maintain certain traditional elements. The two-part ceremony starts with the groom making a formal proposal of marriage to the bride's parents. He asks their permission and then makes an offering of betel leaves and areca nuts. The second part consists of the wedding ceremony, which takes place at an altar set up at the groom's house. The rituals are then followed by a wedding feast and celebration.

To find additional information on various minority groups, find out more about Vietnam's educational system and learn basic Vietnamese phrases, visit vgsbooks.com.

CULTURAL LIFE

Age-old customs and new advances make up Vietnam's culture. In music and theater, classical instruments and songs enjoy wide popularity among modern performers. Painters and architects combine traditional forms and subject matter with contemporary techniques.

Many Vietnamese traditions come from other countries. Centuries of Chinese occupation shaped Vietnam's religious beliefs and artistic styles. The effects of French colonialism are still found in Vietnamese architecture and painting. And other cultures, such as the kingdom of Cham, also left their mark on Vietnam's cultural life.

◎ Religion

Buddhism, practiced in China and India as early as the second century A.D., was adopted in Vietnam during the 1100s. The Chinese form, called Mahayana Buddhism, dominated northern Vietnam. The Indian style, Theravada Buddhism, influenced central and southern Vietnam. Both forms are based on the teachings of the

Buddha (a title meaning "enlightened one"), an Indian prince who lived in the sixth century B.C. Stressing good behavior and moral duties, Buddhism encourages believers to seek perfection through self-knowledge.

Buddhism became Vietnam's official religion in the 1100s. Most Vietnamese also maintained their ancient beliefs, which included worship of their ancestors and respect for a powerful spirit world.

Two religious sects developed in southern Vietnam in the early twentieth century. A faith healer founded Hoa Hao, a reformed Buddhist group that claims about 1.5 million members. This sect emphasizes simplicity of worship and a direct relationship between the individual and the supreme being. The Cao Dai religious sect, which combines several different Asian and European philosophies, has approximately 1 million followers. Cao Dai followers seek divine truth from the works of famous writers, nationalists, scientists, and other popular figures.

The early people of Vietnam believed that everything in nature, living and non-living, had a spirit, a belief called animism. Some spirits were good, some were evil. People avoided using a spirit's name, which could summon the spirit and cause the speaker harm. Modern Vietnamese Buddhists still incorporate elements of animism.

About 10 percent of Vietnamese are Roman Catholic, a faith brought by French missionaries in the 1600s. In 1954, after the country was divided, thousands of North Vietnamese Catholics fled to South Vietnam to avoid harassment. In South Vietnam, President Ngo Dinh Diem, a strong Catholic, persecuted Buddhists and other non-Catholics. Soon after the Communist victory of 1975, the government restricted activities of Catholics and Buddhists throughout Vietnam, fearing they might spread anti-Communist sentiments. Since the mid-1980s, Buddhist temples and Catholic churches have been allowed to hold services and to teach.

Vietnam is also home to Protestants and Muslims (followers of the Islamic religion). Most of the 400,000 Protestants are Montagnards of the Central Highlands. About 50,000 people, mainly Khmer and Chams, follow Islam.

Holidays and Festivals

The people of Vietnam celebrate many religious and nonreligious occasions. The most important religious festival is Tet, a three-day event that falls in late January or early February and marks the arrival of spring and the new year.

The Vietnamese follow special rituals for each day of Tet to ensure good luck for the coming year. Houses are cleaned and decorated with chrysanthemums. Families visit their ancestral altars and family graves to remember the deceased, and on New Year's Eve families offer incense to their ancestors. New Year's Day is ushered in with sweet treats and gifts for the children.

Other important festivals include Trung Thu, or the Mid-Autumn Festival, and Phong Sinh, which celebrates Buddha's birth and death. Lac Long Quan is dedicated to the legendary ancestor of the Vietnamese.

An important national holiday is Liberation Day on April 30, which marks

Chrysanthemums for Tet

The Vietnamese new year, Tet, is celebrated with parades, feasts, and elaborate displays using **fireworks, such as these.**

the 1975 surrender of South Vietnam to North Vietnam. In place of birthdays, the Vietnamese honor deceased relatives and honored people on the anniversary of their death, when gifts and food are placed in temples and homes. People throughout the nation mark the anniversary of Ho Chi Minh's death, for example, on September 2.

If you'd like to find out more about Vietnamese cultural life, go to vgsbooks.com where you'll find links to websites that have information on various cultural customs, food and recipes, holidays and festivals, music, art, literature, and more.

Food

Food has an important place not only during Vietnamese festivals but also in daily life. Although plain rice is a dietary staple, the Vietnamese combine different vegetables, fruits, fish, and meats in a cuisine of great variety. A favorite seasoning is *nuoc mam,* a liquid made from heavily salted fish that have fermented in large vats for months. Cooks combine nuoc mam with sugar, lime juice, vinegar, red pepper flakes, shallots, garlic, and carrots to make *nuoc cham,* also called fish sauce, which is served at almost every meal.

Popular dishes include filleted fish slices broiled over charcoal and frog meat soaked in a thin batter and fried in oil. *Pho,* one of many Vietnamese noodle soups, is popular for breakfast. *Cha gio,* a side dish, is made from thin rice paper filled with finely chopped pork, crab, noodles, mushrooms, eggs, and onions. The ingredients are packed into a tight roll and deep fried. A special seasonal treat often served during Tet is *banh-chung*—small cakes made of rice, yellow beans, pork, scallions, and spices. Before serving banh-chung, cooks wrap the mixture in banana leaves and boil it for eight hours.

PHO

Pho is a noodle soup that is usually eaten at breakfast, but it can be enjoyed any time of day.

3 c. beef or vegetable broth

2 medium onions, chopped

1 tbsp. fresh ginger, minced

1 tsp. salt

2 tbsp. fish sauce, available in most Asian stores (optional)

4 oz. vermicelli or rice noodles

basil, chili peppers, and fresh mint for garnish

Bring broth to a boil and add onion, ginger, salt, and fish sauce. Simmer ten minutes. Add noodles and boil until soft. Remove from heat and garnish with basil, chili peppers, and fresh mint.

Variation: To make *pho bo*, beef noodle soup, add 3 ounces of cooked beef after the noodles have softened. Simmer one minute.

Literature

The oldest Vietnamese writings are folktales meant to be recited. Some of these fables relate the adventures of legendary heroes. Others offer explanations of natural wonders, such as how the water buffalo got its wrinkled skin.

Poetry was the preferred literary form in past centuries. The first major poetic collections were written by court officials and Buddhist monks in the 1100s, after Vietnam gained its independence from China.

Probably the most famous piece of Vietnamese literature is *Kim Van Kieu* (*The Tale of Kieu*), a 3,250-verse poem written by Nguyen Du (1765–1820). This romantic work describes the painful struggles of a beautiful girl named Thuy Kieu. Many Vietnamese can recite whole sections of the poem from memory and sometimes consult passages to help solve personal problems.

Novels, short stories, essays, and dramas became important literary forms in Vietnam in the twentieth century. After 1975, to stop criticism of Communism, the Vietnamese government placed strict controls on the content of published works. Since the establishment of doi moi, government officials have allowed writers much more freedom.

One of the best-selling modern writers is Nguyen Manh Tuan, whose novels often criticize the Communist Party. Another popular writer is Thich Nhat Hanh, a Buddhist monk, who writes popular poems, novels, and folktales. Many of his works, including *A Taste of Earth* and *Hermitage Amongst the Clouds*, have been translated into English.

Music

Vietnam has several distinct styles in music. Classical musicians perform with traditional instruments such as the two-stringed *dan nhi*, similar to a mandolin, and the *dan tranh*, a type of zither with sixteen strings. Other stringed instruments include the *dan bau*, a single-stringed guitar, and the *dan tam* and *ty*, with three and four strings, respectively. Other instruments include bamboo flutes, the *to rung* (a bamboo xylophone), and *trongs* (drums) of various sizes and shapes.

Vietnam's festival tunes, love songs, and lullabies are often sung without accompaniment. Each region of the country and each ethnic group has its own folk melodies. The sad songs of the south, for example, show influences from Cham and India. The boat tunes of Hué, in central Vietnam, glorify heroes of the past.

A common instrument of classical Vietnamese music, **the to rung,** or bamboo xylophone, is played standing up.

Modernized folk music emerged around 1956 and features a combination of Western-style harmonies, traditional and new instruments, and ethnic tunes. Vietnamese teenagers dance to the sounds of pop musicians, both native and foreign. Composers such as Trinh Cong Son and singers such as My Linh have gained widespread popularity among young and old alike.

Theater

Vietnamese popular theater combines singing and instrumental music with poetry, dance, and mime. Performers of *hat cheo*, or popular opera, often use satirical folk songs to criticize the government.

Classical theater *(hat tuong)*, based on Chinese opera, came to Vietnam in the thirteenth century. In these plays, the actors use colors to represent traits such as courage or faithfulness. Musicians accompany each drama, and performers sing their lines.

Cai luong, also known as renovated theater, developed in the 1920s, and combines historical drama with contemporary themes. Short scenes, elaborate sets, and modern music are all elements of cai luong.

Puppet theater is a traditional favorite in Vietnam, where a unique form of the art—water puppetry, or *roi nuoc*—developed centuries ago.

Actors in the cai luong theater stand backstage in makeup and costumes.

Puppeteers stand waist-deep in water as they control their wooden figures with rods and strings hidden beneath the water. As the forms walk gracefully on water, they are surrounded by a stage of sky, trees, and clouds.

Arts and Crafts

Chinese culture played a big role in Vietnam's arts. The Chinese taught the Vietnamese how to make porcelain and other ceramics. Tiles with Chinese designs became a widely used building decoration in the eleventh century. During the Le and Tran dynasties, the Vietnamese created their own distinctive glazes and earthenware designs.

Weaving is another art form with a long history in Vietnam. Hoi An in central Vietnam once led the country in the production of silks, which artisans sold to European traders. Many modern weavers still create cloth on hand looms.

Vietnamese artisans began making shiny lacquerware objects in the 1400s. Artists apply several coats of lacquer to wooden objects

WATER PUPPETRY

Roi nuoc, or water puppetry, probably developed in the Red River Delta as part of a tenth-century agricultural ceremony. According to legend, the art was invented when the stage of a puppet show flooded. Performances include clowns, fireworks, scenes from rural life, legends, and folktales. Once a highly guarded secret, water puppetry nearly died out in the twentieth century. A French organization worked to help revamp the program, and since 1984 this unique art form has once again flourished.

Vietnamese artisans have been creating **lacquerware** objects for nearly six hundred years. Lacquerware boxes, jewelry, paintings, and other works are still prized.

decorated with gold, inlaid pearl, or other materials. Modern crafts-people apply a synthetic resin to produce lacquerware. Traditionally, lacquer came from the sap of the *son* trees.

Painting in Vietnam became more popular in the mid-1900s, when French colonialists opened the Fine Arts College of Indochina (FACI). Many modern painters began painting on silk, an art form that started in ancient China, as a way for Vietnamese artists to distinguish their skills from the French technique of oil painting. Silk painting reached its height in Vietnam between 1925 and 1945, though contemporary painters continue to use it as a medium. Silk painting, which uses people and landscapes as subject matter, is characterized by softness in light and line.

Vietnamese sculpture has a long history that combines foreign influences, including Chinese, Cham, and French. Sculptors' works are mainly found in temples and pagodas and as objects of worship.

Architecture

Vietnam's architecture also shows the influence of the many cultures that have played a part the country's history. The tall, narrow ruins of Cham towers in the Mekong Delta have a distinct Indian influence. These red brick structures have three stories and detailed sculpture inside and out.

Chinese influence can be found in the many pagodas scattered throughout the country and in palace design. The outsides of these pagodas usually feature elaborate ornamental carvings, and the insides reflect the blending of different faiths.

The imperial cities at Hanoi and Hué both show signs of Chinese influence as well. The Hué Citadel was even based on China's Forbidden City in Beijing. Like the Forbidden City, the Hué Citadel has a thick outer wall, which contained the Imperial Enclosure. Within the enclosure was the Forbidden Purple City, the emperor's residence.

French-colonial buildings still stand in Hanoi, Da Nang, and Ho Chi Minh City. Intricate ironwork, pastel colors, and shuttered windows are all elements of this French-colonial style. French architects also built cathedrals for European and Vietnamese Catholics.

Sports and Recreation

While the Vietnamese enjoy sports as a social activity, professional competition is rare. Soccer, however, has become very popular, and professional teams vie for titles in national competition. Nonprofessional athletes play friendly games of table tennis, tennis, and volleyball.

Tae kwon do and other martial arts are also favorites for young and old alike. Some tae kwon do athletes even compete in national and international competitions. In fact, Vietnam won its first-ever Olympic medal in the 2000 games in tae kwon do.

In the cities, people play chess and card games. Kids zip around on scooters and bicycles to meet with their friends. Many young people take music or language lessons or join a youth group for recreation. Theater and movies are also popular in the cities.

People living in the country enjoy games, music, and community gatherings. Television and movies are enjoyed in the areas where they are available.

During the Vietnam War, the South Vietnamese government requested instructors to train its troops in the martial art of **tae kwon do.** The form is still widely practiced all over Vietnam.

THE ECONOMY

After the fighting ended in 1975, Vietnam faced the difficult task of rebuilding its war-damaged economy. To achieve this goal, the Communist government sought to integrate the economy of the south with that of the north. Another priority was to move the south from a free-market economic system to a centrally planned one.

Under a Communist approach, all privately owned land, banks, factories, and businesses become property of the state. This step, called nationalization, allows government officials to control wages and prices and to set production quotas (goals) for industries and farms. By setting quotas, Vietnamese leaders hoped to increase crop yields and the output of consumer goods.

With large amounts of financial aid from the Soviet Union, the Vietnamese government began projects to expand agriculture, to reconstruct roads, and to rebuild factories. To ease the economic burden on cities, the plans included shifting nearly 10 million people from urban areas to new economic zones (NEZs).

In addition to the NEZs, southern farmland was organized into state-owned collectives. Farmers no longer owned their land. In exchange for housing and food, they worked for the state. Southern farmers, who resisted the collectives, did not work very hard to increase their crop yields. They received the same benefits if they worked hard or not. This, in turn, hurt the agricultural sector of Vietnam's economy. In 1981 the government agreed to permit farmers to lease state-owned land in return for a portion of their yield. This allowed the farmers more freedom and allowed them to earn a little more money as well.

By the late 1980s, Vietnam's leaders realized these plans were still not achieving the expected growth. Harvests were low, and consumer goods were still in short supply. In response to these conditions, the government introduced the economic reforms contained in doi moi. This policy relaxed the strict laws governing landownership and provided incentives to encourage investors to start new enterprises. Although these changes stimulated some economic activity, other problems arose.

The Association of Southeast Asian Nations (ASEAN) was established in 1967 to promote political and economic cooperation among nations in the southeast Asia region. Nations belonging to ASEAN work together in areas such as transportation, communications, and agriculture. Policies in finance, trade, and other industries are made to benefit all members of the organization. Member countries are Brunei, Cambodia, Indonesia, Laos, Malaysia, Myanmar, the Philippines, Singapore, Thailand, and Vietnam.

In 1991 the Soviet Union, one of Vietnam's main sources of funding and imports, broke up. This event caused a sharp drop in financial aid and shortages of manufactured items and raw materials. Vietnam's unemployment rate began to climb. At the same time, the U.S. embargo on trade with Vietnam curbed investment and imports.

When the U.S. government lifted the embargo in 1994, Vietnam's economy boomed. Hundreds of small and large businesses sprang up in the major cities. Foreign banks and manufacturing firms set up offices in Vietnam.

By 1997, however, the country's economy had declined due to an underdeveloped infrastructure, such as poor transportation systems, and bureaucratic delays. Foreign investment dropped by more than 50 percent in 1998 and by nearly 65 percent in 1999. Exports also decelerated at that same time, further slowing the economy.

Recognizing that the economy needed a boost, the National Assembly worked out new ways to help promote foreign investments. One of the most important developments was the finalizing of a two-way trade agreement with the United States in 2000. This agreement meant that Vietnam's exports, especially textiles and seafood, would substantially increase. As a result, imports such as consumer goods and fuels also increased, further stimulating the market.

Agriculture

After the Vietnam War and before economic reform policies were in place, Vietnam had trouble feeding all of its people. Government policies set the price of rice and limited the profit of farmers. Famines occurred when rice harvests were poor or when tropical storms damaged fields. The doi moi reforms—which included the removal of price controls—gave farmers reasons to increase their crop yields. As a result, by 1989 Vietnam was able to feed its own population and had become the world's third largest rice exporter, after the United States and Thailand.

The reforms continued to benefit the economy, and Vietnam had become the world's second largest producer of rice by 1997. The nation also found a new cash crop—coffee. By 2000 Vietnam had become the world's second largest producer of coffee.

Farming employs about 69 percent of Vietnam's labor force. The richest soils for rice cultivation are in the Mekong Delta. More than half of Vietnam's rice fields produce two crops each year. By irrigating, some farmers in the Red River Delta can grow three crops annually. High yield rice seeds have also dramatically increased the volume of the rice crop. Farm fertilizers, once imported from the Soviet Union, have further boosted yields.

Many family-run and state-run farms grow nongrain crops—principally corn, beans, sweet potatoes, and cassavas. Smaller holdings produce citrus fruits, bananas, papayas, coconuts, and mangoes. The government encourages the cultivation of these secondary crops to avoid the famines that

DUCKS AND RICE

Duck raising has a long history among Vietnamese farmers because ducks help with growing rice. Farmers release young ducklings into the newly planted paddy of rice seedlings. Ducklings feed on insects, weeds, and snails, cutting down some of the human labor necessary for a healthy crop. Once the rice ears appear, the farmers remove the ducks from the field. During harvesttime, the ducks feed on grains dropped around the fields. When the fields have been harvested, the ducks feed again on the harvested fields. Duck manure helps to fertilize and prepare the field for plowing.

A patient farmer leads a **troop of young ducklings** through a rice paddy. Ducks are used as a kind of natural pesticide by many of Vietnam's rice farmers.

have occurred when rice harvests have been poor. Nevertheless, as rice yields have improved, the production of secondary crops has fallen.

Established during the colonial era, estates devoted to cash-crop farming cultivate peanuts, jute, soybeans, tobacco, rubber trees, tea plants, and coffee shrubs. Money earned from the export of these products allows Vietnam to import needed goods, such as fuels, machinery, and raw materials.

By putting aside public land for grazing, the government has promoted the breeding of more cattle and water buffalo, which are valuable work animals. Larger livestock herds produce a greater supply of manure, which can sometimes substitute for scarce fertilizers. Vietnamese farmers also raise pigs and poultry for food and for sale.

Fishing and Forestry

The Vietnamese government has long encouraged the expansion of the fishing industry, but growth has been slow. The loss of small fishing boats in the 1970s and 1980s, when many Vietnamese used them to flee the country, also hindered the industry's growth.

During the 1990s, however, the government worked to improve the country's fleet and to increase marine production. Equipping boats with

Fishing boats troll the waters near Nha Trang.

Fish vendors crowd the streets of Ho Chi Minh City. Fish is a staple ingredient in Vietnamese cooking and a staple product in the Vietnamese economy.

more powerful motors and better technology, the government encouraged fishers to turn to deep-sea fishing. This not only increased revenues, but it also helped reduce overfishing the depleted coastal waters.

Vietnam's principal fishing areas lie off the coastal lowlands in the South China Sea, where the government has claimed a fishing zone of about 350,000 square miles (906,495 sq. km). Annual catches of crab, shrimp, lobster, squid, and mackerel usually total more than 1.1 million tons (997,913 kg). An interest in fish farming and aquaculture also boosted the industry, and in the late 1990s almost half of Vietnam's seafood exports came from aquaculture.

During the Vietnam War, bombing and chemical spraying destroyed vast stretches of untouched forests. The clearing of land by farmers and the logging of trees to provide fuel has also threatened woodlands. An intensive reforestation project in the 1980s established hardy, fast-growing eucalyptus and acacia trees, whose shade protects more valuable hardwoods that mature slowly. Soldiers, schoolchildren, and teenagers planted hundreds of millions of trees, blanketing thousands of acres of once-deforested land.

The government once hoped that Vietnam's forests could provide building material for markets in Japan, Australia, and Thailand. But as the Vietnamese population grows, the need for wood as a fuel has grown as well. Stands of eucalyptus planted in the 1980s have already been harvested to provide wood. Some Vietnamese activists are urging the replanting of trees in the Mekong Delta to meet future demand.

Despite reforestation efforts, Vietnam's remaining forests are still dwindling. In 1997 the government enacted a ten-year ban on all exports of timber products, except wooden artifacts, in the hopes of preserving the country's natural areas.

Manufacturing and Trade

Although the French and the Japanese established a few industries in Vietnam, manufacturing became more important after the country gained its independence. Industries in the north include government-owned tobacco, tea, and canning factories, while private factories in the south focus on consumer goods such as pharmaceuticals and textiles.

After the country's reunification, the government nationalized all industry. The effects proved disastrous and the Communist Party agreed to allow a small private sector for consumer goods and light industry. Throughout the 1990s, industrial production grew quickly, increasing an average of about 12 percent each year.

Despite a growing manufacturing sector, Vietnam was still importing most consumer goods in the early 1990s. Some arrived as gifts from overseas relatives. Many products smuggled into the country end up on Vietnam's thriving black market, where people buy and sell everything from precious metals to stolen software to endangered plants and animals. People in northern Vietnam crossed the border into China with farm produce and returned with scarce manufactured items.

By 1999 processed food, cigarettes and tobacco, textiles, chemicals, and electronic goods had become the country's main manufactured products. Factories that process agricultural products, such as tea and rubber, are built near the areas in which the crops are raised. Small-scale factories make farm tools, bicycles, and other inexpensive goods. The production of paper, bricks, and glass is growing, but a lack of raw materials has slowed the manufacture of cement and fertilizer.

One of the country's principal mineral exports is petroleum. Vietnam sends most of its petroleum to Japan and Singapore. While the country has one oil refinery, by 1999 Vietnam was still relying on foreign imports of refined petroleum products, such as oil and gasoline.

A typical work-day in Vietnam's cities begins at 7:30 a.m. and ends around 4:30 p.m., six days a week. In the country, farmers begin about 6 a.m. and finish around 5 p.m. Workers rest between 11 a.m. and 2 p.m., the hottest time of day. Farmers work every day during harvesttime.

To stimulate manufacturing, Vietnam actively seeks outside investors. Since 1987 the government has allowed domestic companies to undertake joint projects with foreign firms and has encouraged foreign-owned companies to set up

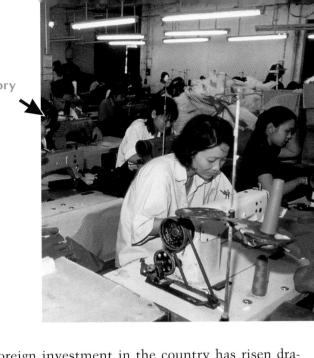

Women work in a factory to create **textiles.**

plants in Vietnam. Foreign investment in the country has risen dramatically in the last few years, and companies from all over the world have started ventures with Vietnamese partners. The growing number of businesses has created a need for factories and office buildings, sparking an increase in construction work. The new firms have also begun to supply more of the consumer goods that Vietnamese citizens are eager, and increasingly able, to purchase.

Since the fall of the Soviet Union, Japan has become Vietnam's principal trading partner. Other active partners are Thailand, Singapore, and Malaysia—all members of ASEAN. Vietnam mainly exports agricultural products, such as rice, coffee, tea, and rubber. The country's chief imports are petroleum, steel, vehicles, machinery, fertilizers, and medicines.

Energy and Mining

Coal, hydroelectric installations, and petroleum are Vietnam's primary sources of domestic energy. In the late 1800s, the French began extracting Vietnam's coal to fuel their merchant fleet, and coal remains one of the country's most important exports. Reserves in northern Vietnam are sizable, and economic planners are working to increase production.

With the help of Soviet funds and technology, Vietnam expanded its energy production in the late 1980s and early 1990s. The government opened several new hydroelectric plants, including a huge facility in northern Vietnam. Additional plants, such as a thermal station in Pha Lai and a nuclear reactor in Da Lat, have also contributed to the increase in energy production.

The Soviets aided the Vietnamese in developing their oil and natural gas industries. In 1986 drilling began in a large oil field in the

South China Sea. Since then, more fields have been discovered in the region. Vietnam allows companies from Britain, Belgium, Canada, and Australia to drill for oil in offshore waters.

The hills of northern Vietnam contain small amounts of many minerals, which have been tapped by French, Japanese, and Soviet companies. West of Cao Bang are deposits of tin and tungsten, both of which Vietnam extracts and exports. Northern Vietnam also provides iron ore and has large reserves of zinc. The country's other mineral resources include antimony, chromium, bauxite, pyrite, and phosphates.

Lack of capital, outdated equipment, and unclear mining laws have all hampered the growth of Vietnam's mining industry. In 1996 the government passed new legislation that made it easier for companies to apply for exploration and mining permits. Preparations to set up a new mining code were started by a conference in 2000. The conference included discussions about updated mining practices and policy reforms, as well as new ways to attract foreign investment.

Transportation

The lack of a good transportation network slows Vietnam's efforts to improve its economy. The main railway lines run between Hanoi and Ho Chi Minh City; between Haiphong and Yunnan, China; and between Hanoi and Guangxi, China. Although the more than 1,700 miles (2,736 km) of track that crosses the country have been largely rebuilt since the

Vietnam War, many sections still need to be modernized.

Vietnam's road system is unable to handle the rising volume of car and truck traffic. The two-lane national artery between Hanoi and Ho Chi Minh City is in disrepair, as is the 60-mile (97 km) road between Hanoi and Haiphong. By 1997 nearly 60,000 miles (96,561 km) of road were covering the country, but only 15,000 miles (24,140 km) were paved. In 1997, recognizing the need to improve and modernize its transportation infrastructure, the government approved construction of a new north-south highway—the largest infrastructural project ever undertaken in the country. It is estimated that construction of the road will be completed by 2012.

Ho Chi Minh City is the principal port of southern Vietnam. In the north, the government is updating and enlarging Haiphong's crowded docks. Other important ports at Nha Trang and Da Nang also clog frequently, and the government is working to update its fleet and harbors.

Asian and European airlines fly into Tan Son Nhut, near Ho Chi Minh City, as well as into Noi Bai airport that

GETTING AROUND

Due to erratic road conditions and limited resources, the Vietnamese have developed diverse modes of transportation. Privately owned automobiles are not common, making public transportation and small vehicles very important. Taxis whiz around city streets, and bus service is available in Hanoi and Ho Chi Minh City. In cities and larger villages, cyclos, bicycles, and mopeds swerve and dodge their way through traffic. In smaller villages, villagers rely on bicycles, boats (in coastal regions and along the rivers), and foot power. For the long haul, a train network dating back to the colonial period covers about 2,000 miles (3,219 km) between major cities and coastal towns.

Boys run alongside a train traveling from Hanoi to Ho Chi Minh City.

recently opened outside of Hanoi. In 1997 the government announced that abandoned wartime airstrips would be repaired and put into service by 2010.

Vietnam Airlines, the national carrier, provides service to eighteen countries. The airline, which once relied solely on old Soviet passenger planes, has Boeing 737s and Boeing 777s in its fleet.

Tourism

Despite poor road, rail, and air links, travelers are flocking to Vietnam. Some are businesspeople investigating trade and manufacturing opportunities. Others are Vietnamese-born foreigners—called Viet Kieu—and children of Vietnamese emigrants who come to see relatives or to invest in local businesses. A number of tourists are Vietnam War veterans from the United States who revisit old battlefields. In need of foreign currency, the Vietnamese government welcomes them all. The hotel industry has boomed with the wave of visitors. Cafés, nightclubs, and restaurants have reopened, especially in Ho Chi Minh City and Hanoi.

Guided by former soldiers, tourists can explore the Cu Chi Tunnels, an underground network of passageways built by the North Vietnamese army during French occupation, and later used by the Viet Cong to infiltrate South Vietnam. Ancient temples, Buddhist shrines, and

Tour guides lead tourists through the **Cu Chi Tunnels,** a network of underground tunnels built by the North Vietnamese army.

Cham ruins draw people interested in Vietnam's earlier history. Mountain resorts, such as Da Lat, offer cool temperatures and breathtaking scenery. Broad beaches, especially near Da Nang and Nha Trang, attract foreign guests as well as Vietnamese vacationers. In Hanoi visitors can enjoy the city's French-colonial architecture or view the embalmed remains of Ho Chi Minh in a huge, Soviet-built mausoleum. Hué presents historic tombs and buildings from the period of Vietnam's last independent emperors.

Visit vgsbooks.com for up-to-date information about Vietnam's economy and a converter with the current exchange rate where you can learn how many dong are in a U.S. dollar.

The Future

The new millennium ushered in a new era for Vietnam. The country's new market economy, despite its early setbacks, has sparked economic growth with foreign investments and overseas trade. Billboards in Hanoi and Ho Chi Minh City advertise the latest electronics equipment. Small businesses and bustling farmers' markets that crowd city streets are signs of the country's escalating free market.

In 2000 the government announced plans to develop the country's information technology (IT) to modernize its economy, culture, and defense system. The main goal of this plan is to close the socio-economic gap between Vietnam and industrialized countries by opening the country to the global market. The country is also working to establish a national computer network to provide business information to the general public. Also in 2000, Vietnam's first stock market was established, another sign of the country's economic progress.

Despite these advances, the continuing problems of bureaucratic delays and a poor transportation network pose obstacles to progress. Vietnam's biggest challenge, however, is to balance its economic goals with its political ideals. The Communist government must decide how much free competition to allow in the country and how soon to allow it.

The nation's leaders hesitate to surrender control of Vietnam's economy and resources. Officials also fear that new problems—political unrest, higher crime rates, and a larger disparity between rich and poor—will spread along with capitalism. The coming years will determine whether Vietnam can realize its economic potential while retaining the degree of government control it has had in the past.

3000–1000 B.C.	Nomadic tribes settle in the Red River Delta region.
800s B.C.	The Dong-son culture emerges.
500s B.C.	Sa Hyunh culture influences pottery and jewelry techniques in the Mekong Delta.
250 B.C.	An Duong Vuong establishes Au Lac, the region's first centralized kingdom.
207 B.C.	The Chinese conquer the Red River Delta. Chinese commander Zhao Tuo names the kingdom Nam Viet.
A.D. 39	The Trung sisters lead a Vietnamese rebellion against the Chinese.
43	China's forces defeat the Trung sisters.
300–400s	Trade between Southeast Asia and India flourishes.
700	Chams erect temples at My Son.
939	Ngo Quyen wins Nam Viet's independence from China.
1009	Vietnam's Ly dynasty is founded. The country is renamed Dai Viet.
1100s	Buddhism becomes Vietnam's official religion.
1400s	Artisans begin making lacquerware objects.
1407	China retakes Dai Viet.
1427	Le Loi defeats Chinese forces and establishes the Le dynasty.
1471	Vietnam conquers Cham.
1627	Quoc ngu alphabet is created.
1771–1787	The Tay Son rebellion unites northern and southern Vietnam under one ruler.
CA. 1800	Nguyen Du composes *Kim Van Kieu*.
1802	Nguyen Anh establishes the Nguyen dynasty. He renames himself Emperor Gia Long.
1805	Construction begins on the Hué Citadel.
1867	French troops seize southern Vietnam, known as Cochin China.
1883	The French take over central and northern Vietnam and form the Union of Indochina.
1926	Ngo Minh Chieu founds the Cao Dai sect.

1930   Ho Chi Minh creates the Indochinese Communist Party (ICP).

1939   Hoa Hao religious sect is established.

1940   ICP leaders flee to southern China and form the Viet Minh, an organization dedicated to overthrowing French rule in Vietnam.

1944   Van Cao composes "Tien Quan Ca" (Forward, Soldiers!), Vietnam's national anthem.

1945   Ho Chi Minh heads a new government in Hanoi.

1946   The First Indochina War starts.

1954   Viet Minh forces defeat the French. The country is divided into North Vietnam and South Vietnam.

1956   Modern folk music develops.

1957   North Vietnam guerrillas attack South Vietnam.

1965   The United States sends combat troops to help South Vietnam.

1969   U.S. president Richard Nixon begins withdrawing troops from Vietnam. Ho Chi Minh dies.

1975   Vietnam is reunited as the Socialist Republic of Vietnam.

1978   Vietnam invades Cambodia.

1979   China invades northern Vietnam and cuts off aid to the country.

1986   The government introduces doi moi economic reforms.

1991   Vietnam withdraws its troops from Cambodia.

1994   The United States lifts its trade embargo against Vietnam.

2000   The government announces plans to develop Vietnam's information technology (IT) industry. The country's first stock market opens.

2002   In national elections, the Vietnamese Communist Party won 90 percent of the seats in the National Assembly.

COUNTRY NAME Socialist Republic of Vietnam

AREA 128,066 square miles (204,906 sq. km)

MAIN LANDFORMS Annamite Mountains, Central Highlands, Mekong Delta, Red River Delta, Tonkin Lowlands

HIGHEST POINT Fan Si Pan, 10,312 feet (3,143 m) above sea level

LOWEST POINT Sea level

MAJOR RIVERS Ca River, Da River, Ma River, Mekong River, Red River, Thai Binh River

ANIMALS Asian elephants, Asiatic black bears, bantengs, concolor gibbons, duoc langurs, Indian elephants, Javan rhinos, koupreys, leopards, macaques, muntjac deer, serows, tigers

CAPITAL CITY Hanoi

OTHER MAJOR CITIES Ho Chi Minh City (Saigon), Hanoi, Haiphong, Da Nang, Hué, Nha Trang

OFFICIAL LANGUAGE Vietnamese

MONETARY UNIT Dong. 10 *hao* = 1 dong; 100 *xu* = 10 hao.

Currency Fast Facts

VIETNAMESE CURRENCY

Vietnam's monetary unit is the dong, a paper currency. (1 dong=10 hao=100 xu.) There are coins of 1, 2, and 5 xu, as well as notes of 5 xu. Hao notes come in denominations of 1, 2, and 5 hao. Dong notes range from small denominations of 1, 2, 5, and 10 to larger denominations of 500, 10,000, and 100,000.

Vietnam's current flag was created in 1945, when the Indochinese Communist Party declared the country's independence. A yellow five-pointed star stands in the center of a red flag, both symbols of Communism. The five points of the star symbolize farmers, workers, scholars, soldiers, and young people. In 1955 the flag was officially adopted by the government.

Vietnam's national anthem, "Tien Quan Ca" ("Forward, Soldiers!"), was written by composer Van Cao (1923–1995). He published the lyrics on the first art page of *Doc Lap,* the newspaper where he worked, and the song instantly became popular. In 1946 North Vietnam adopted "Tien Quan Ca" as its national anthem, and in 1976 the song became the anthem for the reunited country. The lyrics celebrate the country's fight for independence. The first two verses are printed below.

Tien Quan Ca (Forward, Soldiers!)

Soldiers of Vietnam, we go forward,
With the one will to save our Fatherland,
Our hurried steps are sounding on the long and arduous road.
Our flag, red with the blood of victory, bears the spirit of our country.

The distant rumbling of the guns mingles with our marching song.
The path to glory passes over the bodies of our foes.
Overcoming all hardships, together we build our resistance bases.
Ceaselessly for the people's cause let us struggle,
Let us hasten to the battlefield!
Forward! All together advancing!
Our Vietnam is strong, eternal.

For a link where you can listen to Vietnam's national anthem, "Tien Quan Ca" (Forward, Soldiers!), go to vgsbooks.com.

Vietnamese names consist of a family name, a middle name (which is not always used), and a given name. When written in the traditional style, the family name appears first. For example, Ho Chi Minh is from the Ho family, his middle name is Chi, and his given name is Minh. The following Vietnamese names are written in traditional order, with family name first.

Famous People

GIA LONG (1762–1820) Gia Long proclaimed himself emperor of Vietnam in 1802, a position he held until his death in 1820. Gia Long established the Nguyen dynasty (1802–1945) and under his rule, Vietnam was reunited under one government. His reign was marked by conservative policies, isolation from European influence, and legal reforms. The Citadel in Hué was built under his direction.

HO CHI MINH (1890–1969) Ho Chi Minh was a political leader who organized Vietnamese nationalists in the mid-1900s. Born Nguyen That Thanh, he changed his name to Ho Chi Minh, which means "He Who Enlightens," around 1940. Ho helped Vietnam gain its independence from French occupation, and he established the Indochinese Communist Party in 1930.

KHANH LY (b. 1945) Khanh Ly is a singer who began her career at fourteen when she won second place in a radio talent search for children. Around 1967 Ly became the first Vietnamese woman to headline her own shows. Most of her songs encourage peace, and she performed for troops at the front lines during the Vietnam War. In 1969 Khanh Ly became the first Vietnamese singer to travel and perform in Europe and the United States.

KIEU CHINH (b. 1939) Kieu Chinh is an actress who has worked in international films for more than forty years. She has appeared in more than seventy television shows and movies. Her most famous movies include *M*A*S*H*, *Hamburger Hill*, and *The Joy Luck Club*. In 1990 the U.S. House of Representatives named her "Refugee of the Year." Chinh won an Emmy for her documentary *Kieu Chinh: A Journey Home*.

LAAM TOUI (1940–2000) Laam Toui was one of Vietnam's earliest movie stars. Toui attended Vietnam Cinematography College from 1959 to 1962. He starred in *Two Soldiers* shortly after graduating and became a national star. Toui starred in twenty films, and his works include *On the Road to Homeland*, *The 17th Parallel*, and *Days and Nights*. In 1974 he won a Gold Award at the International Film Festival in Moscow for his role in *The Wild Field*, which also won the Best Film Award.

NGO TAT TO (1894–1954) Ngo Tat To was a writer who described the plight of Vietnam's poor. Ngo's articles dealt with controversial topics, such as freedom of speech. His most famous work is the novel *Fading Lamp.* He was posthumously awarded the Ho Chi Minh Prize by the State Council in Ho Chi Minh City.

NGO VAN CHIEU (1878–1926) Ngo Van Chieu founded the Cao Dai sect, a religion that combines elements of Confucianism, Buddhism, Taoism, and Catholicism. In 1919 Ngo was a minor official living in Phu Quoc, an island in the Gulf of Thailand, when he claimed to have a revelation. In 1925 he became the sect's first pope and worked to spread Cao Daism across the nation.

NGUYEN DU (1765–1820) Nguyen Du was a poet and diplomat whom modern Vietnamese still consider their national poet. Born to a scholarly family in Tien-Dien, Nguyen passed the traditional exams to become a mandarin. He served as a provincial administrator and diplomat to the court of Emperor Gia Long, and in 1813 he was appointed Grand Chancellor of the Empire. During his service to the court, he composed his most famous poem, *Kim Van Kieu.*

NGUYEN TUE (b. 1962) Nguyen Tue fled Vietnam as a refugee in 1978. By 1988 he had earned seven degrees from the Massachusetts Institute of Technology (MIT) in seven years, breaking the institute's record and earning him the nickname Super Scholar. His degrees include five bachelor's degrees (physics, computer science, electronics, mathematics, and atomic engineering) and a master's degree and doctorate in atomic engineering. Nguyen works for IBM in Virginia.

TRAN DU (b. 1941) Tran Du is a businessman and the founder of VANCO Food Supermarket chains. At age eight, Tran helped support his family by selling cakes and newspapers along the streets of his village. When he and his family moved to the United States in 1979, he created an import company that he named VANCO. Because of his extensive community service, the U.S. Congress honored Tran with the 1990 Business Person of the Year Award.

TRAN HIEU NGAN (b. 1974) Tran Hieu Ngan is the first Vietnamese athlete to win an Olympic medal. Ngan won a silver medal for the women's 125 pound (57 kg) class in tae kwon do in the 2000 Summer Olympic Games in Sydney, Australia. Ngan, who was born in the small town of Tuy Hoa, started tae kwon do when she was fourteen. She won her first national championship in 1994, received a gold medal at the 1996 Southeast Asian Games, and won a bronze medal at the 1998 Asian Games.

TRUONG VINH KY (1837–1898) Truong Vinh Ky, who was born in Vinh Thanh village, wrote 118 works of literature and approximately 20 unfinished novels. He was the first famous writer to use quoc ngu for writing and was an editor for *Giadinh,* the first newspaper in Vietnamese.

THE CITADEL Built by the Emperor Gia Long in the nineteenth century, the Citadel houses the Imperial City, which was modeled after Beijing's Forbidden City and includes the royal palaces and several museums. It is located in Hué.

CU CHI TUNNELS This tunnel network, running from Ben Dinh to Ben Duoc, became legendary during the Vietnam War for its role as the underground home of the Viet Cong.

CUC PHUONG NATIONAL PARK This park, located in the Ninh Bihn Province, was dedicated by Ho Chi Minh in 1963. It features prehistoric caves, hot springs, and the Endangered Primate Rescue Center.

EMPEROR OF JADE PAGODA This Chinese temple in Ho Chi Minh City is filled with colorful statues representing figures from Buddhist and Taoist traditions.

HISTORY MUSEUM The artifacts in this museum in Hanoi reflect the country's development from prehistoric times to its independence from France. Highlights include exhibits from the Dong-son culture and an eleventh century statue of Buddha.

HO CHI MINH'S MAUSOLEUM This glass sarcophagus is the final resting place of Ho Chi Minh. The mausoleum, one of Hanoi's most popular sites, has become a pilgrimage site.

MUSEUM OF VIETNAMESE WOMEN This museum in Hanoi offers a unique perspective on the country's history. One of the highlights of the museum is a collection of ethnic costumes worn by the fifty-four minority groups living in Vietnam.

REVOLUTIONARY MUSEUM Housed in the former Gia Long Palace in Ho Chi Minh City, this museum uses photographs and artifacts to chronicle the Vietnamese struggle for independence.

ROYAL TOMBS Visitors to Hué can check out the mausoleums of the Nguyen dynasty rulers, as well as the Royal Arena and the Temple of Heaven—once one of the most important religious sites in Vietnam.

VAN MIEU (TEMPLE OF LITERATURE) Founded in 1070, this temple in Hanoi was dedicated to Confucius to honor scholars and their literary achievements. The temple is a good example of traditional Vietnamese architecture.

WAR CRIMES MUSEUM Probably the most popular attraction in Ho Chi Minh City, this museum recounts the horrors of modern warfare.

boat people: Vietnamese refugees, mostly ethnic minorities and southern Vietnamese, who fled the country in small boats after the Communist victory in 1975

Buddhism: a religion that originated in India in about 500 B.C. Buddhism teaches that the way to enlightenment is through meditation and self-knowledge.

Communism: a theory of common ownership; a system of government in which the government controls industry and agriculture

Confucianism: a philosophy based on the teachings of Confucius (551–478 B.C.) that spells out civil, family, and social duties

doi moi: Vietnam's economic reform policy, which allows for some privatization of businesses and industries. The policy of doi moi was adopted in 1986.

guerrilla: a member of a lightly armed military group that uses quick raids from hidden bases to strike against a larger military force

mandarin: a scholar who passed a series of examinations to become an administrative official. Mandarins ran the country's central administration from about 1470 to the early 1900s.

military junta: a group that seizes power of a government after a revolution

monsoon: a seasonal wind that typically blows from the southwest and is often accompanied by heavy rains

nationalist: a person or group dedicated to the advancement of or independence of their country

paddy: a rice field that may be farmed either wet or dry

pagoda: a tower-shaped Buddhist temple where people worship

trade embargo: a government restriction that limits or prohibits commerce between specified nations

Viet Cong (VC): stands for Vietnamese Communists; one of the guerrilla forces that fought for control of the country in the mid-1900s

Viet Minh: stands for Viet Nam Doc Lap Dong Minh (League of Independence of Vietnam); founded by Ho Chi Minh in 1941 to fight for Vietnam's independence from the French.

Selected Bibliography

Cole, Wendy. *Vietnam.* **Philadelphia: Chelsea House, 1999.**
Cole's book provides a good, basic overview of the country and the people.

Duiker, William. *Historical Dictionary of Vietnam.* **Metuchen, NJ: Scarecrow Press, 1989.**
This work offers an introduction to the country.

Europa Year World Book. **Vol. 2. London: Europa Publications Ltd., 2001.**
The article covering Vietnam includes recent events, vital statistics, and economic information.

Fincher, E. B. *The Vietnam War.* **New York: Watts, 1980.**
Fincher presents a context for the Vietnam War, as well as its unforeseen complications and consequences.

Kamm, Henry. *Dragon Ascending: Vietnam and the Vietnamese.* **New York: Arcade Publishing, 1996.**
Learn about the country through the eyes of its people.

Karnow, Stanley. *Vietnam: A History.* **New York: Viking Press, 1983.**
This account of the Vietnam War gives the war a deeper historical context, including Chinese and French occupations of the country and the rise of nationalism in the twentieth century.

Nhan Dan Online. **February 2, 2002.**
Website: <http://www.nhandan.org.vn/> (February 2, 2002).
The online version of Vietnam's *Nhan Dan* newspaper features articles covering recent developments in the country's social and political arenas.

Population Reference Bureau. **May 2001.**
Website: <http://www.prb.org> (December 5, 2001).
The bureau offers current population figures, vital statistics, land area, and more. Special articles cover the latest environmental and health issues that concern each country.

Rowthorn, Chris, et al. *South-East Asia on a Shoestring.* **11th ed. Melbourne, Australia: Lonely Planet Publications, 2001.**
A short but full chapter on Vietnam covers history, regional facts, and major sights to see.

SarDesai, D. R. *Vietnam: The Struggle for National Identity.* **Boulder, CO: Westview Press, 1992.**
This work offers readers an in-depth look at the country's postwar reconstruction and its contemporary politics.

Seah, Audrey. *Vietnam.* **New York: Marshall Cavendish, 1994.**
Part of the *Cultures of the World* series, this book pays special attention to such topics as language, festivals, and the arts.

Shalant, Phyllis. *Look What We've Brought You from Vietnam.* **Parsippany, NJ: Julian Messner, 1998.**
This book features games, crafts, stories, and other cultural activities from Vietnam.

Statesman's Yearbook. **London: Macmillan, 2000.**

This resource features information about the country's historical events, industry and trade, climate and topography, as well as suggestions for further reading.

Trien Thi Choi. ***The Food of Vietnam.*** **North Claredon, VT: Periplus, 1997.**

Learn about Vietnamese cuisine and cooking techniques in this colorful cookbook.

Viet Nam. **n.d.**

Website: <http://www.viettouch.com/> **(December 28, 2001).**

This comprehensive website offers information about Vietnam's art and history. Special features include a history timeline, a Who's Who section, and an extensive discussion of the country's music and arts.

The World Factbook. **January 1, 2001.**

Website: <http://www.cia.gov/cia/publications/factbook/geos/vm.html> **(December 5, 2001).**

This website features up-to-date information about the people, land, economy, and government of Vietnam. Transnational issues are also briefly covered.

World Gazetteer. **January 1, 2001.**

Website: <http://www.gazetteer.de/index.htm> **(December 28, 2001).**

The online World Gazetteer offers population information about cities, towns, and places for all countries, including their administrative divisions.

Galt, Margot Fortunato. *Stop this War! American Protest of the Conflict in Vietnam.* **Minneapolis: Lerner Publications Company, 2000.**
Learn about the reaction among America's youth to the Vietnam War during the 1960s and 1970s.

Garland, Sherry. *Children of the Dragon: Selected Tales from Vietnam.* **New York: Harcourt, 2001.**
This book is a collection of six traditional folktales from Vietnam.

Garland, Sherry. *Song of the Buffalo Boy.* **New York: Harcourt, 1994.**
Seventeen-year-old Loi, an Amerasian living in Vietnam, runs away to Saigon to avoid an arranged marriage.

Kalman, Bobbie. *Vietnam: The Land.* **New York: Crabtree, 2002.**
This book covers the geography of Vietnam and includes full-color maps.

Millett, Sandra. *The Hmong of Southeast Asia.* **Minneapolis: Lerner Publications Company, 2002.**
The Hmong are one of the largest ethnic groups in Vietnam. This book explores aspects of their culture, from dress to meal preparation.

Nguyen, Chi. *Cooking the Vietnamese Way.* **Minneapolis: Lerner Publications Company, 2002.**
Learn more about Vietnamese cooking and culture, including traditional dishes and festival foods.

O'Connor, Karen. *Vietnam.* **Minneapolis: Carolrhoda Books, Inc., 1999.**
This book explores the major landforms, ethnic groups, culture, and geography of Vietnam.

Pomerantz, Charlotte. *The Princess and the Admiral.* **New York: Feminist Press, 1992**
This retelling of a Vietnamese folktale is set in the thirteenth century. Clever Princess Mat Mat uses her wits to defeat a Mongol admiral.

Quang, Nhuong Huynh. *The Land I Lost: Adventures of a Boy in Vietnam.* **New York: HarperTrophy, 1986.**
This collection of short stories describes the childhood of Nhuong Huynh Quang, who grew up in Vietnam's highlands.

Springstubb, Tricia. *The Vietnamese Americans.* **San Diego, CA: Lucent Books, 2001.**
This book describes the obstacles and achievements of many Vietnamese who left their homeland to settle in the United States.

TIMEasia.com
Website: <http://www.time.com/time/asia/>
This online version of *Time* magazine focuses on current events happening in Asia and the Pacific.

Further Reading and Websites

vgsbooks.com
Website: <http://www.vgsbooks.com>

Visit vgsbooks.com, the homepage of the Visual Geography Series®. You can get linked to all sorts of useful on-line information, including geographical, historical, demographic, cultural, and economic websites. The vgsbooks.com site is a great resource for late-breaking news and statistics.

Viet Nam
Website: <http://www.viettouch.com/>

This comprehensive website offers information about Vietnam's art and history. Special features include a history timeline, a Who's Who section, and an extensive discussion of the country's music and arts.

Whelan, Gloria. *Goodbye Vietnam.* New York: Random House, 1993.

Thirteen-year-old Mail is forced to flee from her village in the Mekong Delta when her family learns that government soldiers have an order to apprehend her father.

White, Ellen Emerson. *The Journal of Patrick Seamus Flaherty: United States Marine Corps, Khe Sanh, Vietnam, 1968.* New York: Scholastic, 2002.

This fictitious diary follows young Patrick as he joins the U.S. Marine Corps in 1967. Shortly after basic training, he finds himself in the middle of the conflict in Vietnam.

Captions for photos appearing on cover and chapter openers:

Cover: This serene water garden is located in the city of Hué.

pp. 4–5 A woman plants rice, one of Vietnam's most important crops.

pp. 8–9 A majestic view of the Ma River near Ba Thuoc

pp. 18–19 The Cham Empire built the temple complex at My Son in the A.D. 700s. Crumbling stone ruins are all that remain of the once-magnificent buildings.

pp. 38–39 A Thai girl, a member of one of Vietnam's ethnic minorities, wears traditional dress.

pp. 44–45 In Tay Nihn, a group of Cao Dai worshipers prays together. Followers of the Cao Dai philosophy seek divine truth from a combination of Asian and European philosophers.

pp. 54–55 Factory workers at a Mercedes Benz plant in Ho Chi Minh City work on an assembly line. Manufacturing consumer goods is a small but growing sector of Vietnam's economy.

Photo Acknowledgments
© A. Ghazzal/TRIP, p. 4–5; PresentationMaps.com, pp. 6, 11; © Russell Ciochon, pp. 8–9, 21, 31, 53; © Nevada Wier, pp. 10, 38–39, 40; © Steve Raymer/CORBIS, p. 12; © Michael S. Yamashita/CORBIS, p. 13; © H. Bower/TRIP, pp. 16, 49; © T. Bognar/TRIP, pp. 18-19, 24; © Brian A. Vikander/CORBIS, p. 22; © Hulton-Deutsch Collection/CORBIS, p. 26; National Archives, pp. 28 (Photo No. 306-PS-55-13670), 29 (Photo No. 127–GVB-A371421); © Owen Franken/CORBIS, p. 34; © Reuters NewMedia Inc./CORBIS, p. 35; © AFP/CORBIS, pp. 36-37; © Tim Page/CORBIS, pp. 41, 62–63; © A. Tovy/TRIP, p. 42 (top); © E. Young/TRIP, p. 42 (bottom); © R. Nichols/TRIP, pp. 44–45, 47, 52; © J. Wakelin/TRIP, p. 46; © Catherine Karnow/CORBIS, p. 50; © W. Jacobs/TRIP, p. 51; © Ask Images/TRIP, pp. 54–55, 61;© Caroline Penn/CORBIS, p. 57; © G. Stokoe/TRIP, p. 58; © M. Azavedo/TRIP, p. 59; © R. Belbin/TRIP, p. 64; www.banknotes.com, p. 68; Laura Westlund, p. 69.

Cover photo: SeaQuest Cruises. Back cover photo: NASA.